Live It

Riding the Highs and Lows
of a Cross Country Dream

Published by Fifth Estate Media, Maitland, Florida

www.nonfictionpublish.com

Printed in the United States of America

DESIGN BY KIRK DOUPONCE
DogEared Design

AUTHOR PHOTO BY JULIE FLETCHER
www.juliefletcherphotography.com

MAP ILLUSTRATION
Samantha Heinrich

The author is grateful for copyrighted excerpts of material from Hope for The Warriors®

U.S. Library of Congress cataloging publication data:
Draper, Tracy

Live It: Riding the Highs and Lows
of a Cross Country Dream

Acknowledgements

While it is impossible to list every person who helped make this adventure materialize, there was a large group of cross-country enablers who aided the success of the Ride Across USA. Many thanks for your support.

California – Sarah Duerr, Scott Hillman, David Coleman, Hook Community Center

Arizona – Rosie Newbold, Roger Ely, Stephen Bingall, Matthew J. Broehm Post 12128 VFW Williams, St. John's Episcopal-Lutheran Church, Anthony at Absolute Bikes, Flagstaff, Dennehotso Chapter, Carmelia Blackwater, Art, Frank and our teenage "wild ride guide"

Colorado – Bayfield Baptist Church, Debbie Renfro, Herb Rodriguez, Front Rangers Cycling Team, Cindy Keenan, Jeff Johnson, Adrienne Atencio, High Valley Community Center, The Windsor Hotel, Steve and Connie Whitehead, Regan and Kodi Whitehead, Joanne Kaufman, Tina Killinen, First United Methodist Church of Salida, James Chiles, Sundance Mountain Resort, Bill Clark, Koshare Kiva Museum

Kansas – Joe Gould, Syracuse Christian Academy, Black Bison Pub, William Royer, Randi Clifford, Dodge City YMCA, Wanda, Josh Bell, Kingman Christian Church, Kingman Chamber of Commerce, John Wolfe, Shondra Kostner, Ronnie Fankhauser, G&S Catering, Kristie Williams, Matt Childers, Augusta Travel Bureau, Parsons Recreation and Community Center, Arianna Garrison, Parsons Recreation Commission, Gary Crissman

Missouri – Max Springer, Mayor John Eden, The MARC of Mount Vernon

Tennessee – Steve Guttery, Dyersburg Chamber of Commerce, Rachel Baker, Tennessee River Museum, New Hope Pentecostal Church, Pastor Larry Adair

Alabama – Bea Jai Merriam, Phyllis Clopton, Capt. Kyle Comfort Foundation, Joel and Nancy Denney, Mellow Mushroom of Oxford, Curtis Cupp, Oxford Fire Department

Georgia – First Baptist Church Columbus, Cynthia Bradshaw, Michele Moulton, Ken Wheeler, Diane Proctor, Sherwood Baptist Church, Dick and Ivy Sceals, Pecan City Pedalers

Florida – John and Pam Hunt, Julz Bennett, Nathaniel Dixon, Gale Bellew, Laurie Manning, Edd Holder & Associates, Tamsett Electric, Harris Air Conditioning, O'Keefes, Moons & Balloons Photography, Akers Media Group, Lou Ann, D2 Cycling, Jeff and Laura Stephens, volunteers at both Warrior Rides, Sun Cycles, Niagara Bottling Company, Mary Bevins, Golds Gym Mount Dora, The Marks Law Firm, Animal Medical Center, Mike Pettis Realty, my personal training clients, Sabbath Grace Fellowship, Joanne and Rally Bacchus

Financial Supporters
Through the Indiegogo campaign and the Ride Across USA fundraising page on H4W's site

The Team
Scott Manning, Marion Kusters, Clay Smith, Ruth D'Aiuto, Bill Bellew, Keith Sherrick and Ed Bennett

My Family
If not for the incredible support each of you displayed, this dream would not have come true. Billy – you share in the success of this by your undying support. You sacrificed more than anyone. Our children: Chrissy, Jordan, Jay and Suzie, for your care and concern during the planning and execution of the Ride and for being proud of me at the end. Mom, who said "You're crazy" when I told you of my desire to do this. Perhaps you were right but you believed in me anyway. Dad, who said to me, "I think you should." Jeff, Jackie and Cameron, for making a long drive to spend a short time with us in Del Norte. Leigh and Blair, for driving over a thousand miles and giving precious vacation time to be a part of this.

Live It

Riding the Highs and Lows
of a Cross Country Dream

A small-town fitness coach dreamed
of riding her bike across America.

TRACY DRAPER

And the dream continues with a ride and photo with
Jens Voigt, winner of Tour de France stages and
distinguished member of Trek pro racing teams.

Dedication

To my husband, who enabled the dream
To my parents, who supported the dream
To my children, who are a part of the dream
and
To those who want to Live It now.

Table of Contents

Introduction

"Each of us are born with the responsibility of living out our lives by helping others. A life lived only for self is shallow and unfulfilling." (Unknown)

In 2010, one of my husband's closest friends was diagnosed with a rare, aggressive form of non-Hodgkin's lymphoma. Ricky is a man of great faith, an intense ability to love and passionately live life. How could this happen to him? He did not smoke, drink or do anything that would hurt his body, except indulge in a bit of ice cream occasionally. He lived clean, loved much and was a bright spot in everyone's day.

Ricky's career was in the medical field -- radiation oncology. At work one day, he started coughing and having difficulty breathing. He had a chest CT scan that revealed a baseball-sized mass between his lungs. Doctors immediately ran tests and scheduled treatments. They told him it would be a long fight but that there was a chance he could be saved.

My husband, Billy, spent many of his lunch hours at Ricky's bedside, trying to encourage him and give him hope. Ricky was fading and his usual, upbeat personality had been usurped by this ravenous disease. Over the months of chemo, we witnessed his hair loss, his normally vibrant eyes dimmed and his body withered away from 160 pounds to a frail 138 pounds.

His beautiful wife, Marta, was a constant source of strength for him. Their college-age daughter came to visit daily. When Billy and I stopped by for a short visit after church one day, I was deeply saddened by what I saw: a worn-down, weakened, dying man. The timeframe was 2012, late summer. I had been training very hard for an ultra-distance AquaBike race in Clermont, Florida, and I told Ricky that I was going to dedicate the race to him. Somehow his sickly lips formed a slight smile and I could tell that it meant something to him.

Days passed and Ricky grew worse. He told Billy that he could feel the life slipping from him. His faith was never shaky. He was afraid, yet he believed God was instructing him to get off chemo and try a natural cure. Of course, we were all skeptical -- except for Ricky. He was convinced.

Infused by his own belief that this is how he was to battle cancer, he summoned his wife, daughter and doctors for a new treatment plan. Somehow he had enough strength to make this happen. While his doctors advised against it, he insisted, "Chemo is killing me. I have no other choice but to try this." He knew he would perish if he continued more rounds of liquid death.

During this time, Billy and I had hoped for a good turnout for our dying friend. Perhaps I could say we dreamed of it, because we did not have the faith to fully believe that it would happen. I had only seen this type of miraculous healing in a friend in the late 1990s and she, too, was convinced that God was going to do a mighty work. But I have also seen -- with much more frequency -- people claim a healing that did not end the way we had hoped it would. So I prayed for Ricky's healing and quietly wondered if it was to turn out the way we wanted it to.

I continued to train hard for this race. Each training ride became a mission with Ricky's condition in mind. While my legs ached and lungs burned from pushing hard and fast up the central Florida hills, I could only guess what Ricky was feeling. When a two-mile training swim left me tired, my thoughts turned to Ricky and whether he would ever be able to swim again. Weeks passed and race day drew near. Two and a half months to go until the race.

As my training continued, Ricky was discharged from the hospital and spent weeks at home to rebuild his immune system so that he could go to an alternative cancer treatment center in south Florida. He was a very sick man indeed but was beginning to feel life re-enter his body as the effects of chemo dissipated. The tumor had been eradicated by chemotherapy and the cancer cells were absent in his system, according to the lab reports. The latest scan and lab reports showed no evidence of disease; however, his physician was concerned about any cells that might be lingering causing a recurrence in the future.

In September, he was able to attend a three week session under medical supervision at Hippocrates Health Institute where he learned about natural nutrition and holistic healing of the body, mind and spirit. It did not take long for this life-giving nutrition to take effect and he started feeling alive again -- and hopeful. He had just taken a huge step to try to save his life, and it appeared to be successful. It was now just a few weeks before the race, and Ricky had just graduated from the treatment center with a new outlook on life. He was drinking daily shots of wheatgrass and even growing trays of it in his kitchen. He had gained a few pounds and his strength was returning. Billy visited him and came home to report that Ricky was returning to the same ol' friend he knew from the time before cancer invaded his body. Ricky would not be strong enough to meet us at the finish line, but I knew he and his family would be cheering me on from their home in Orlando.

The Great Floridian race is an annual event that brings contestants from all over the United States and many other countries each fall. It is known for the difficult bike portion that spans 112 miles with thousands of feet of climbing spread across the miles. There are different races staged throughout the day: triathlon, open-water swim and aquabike. My particular race began at 7:25 am and would conclude sometime in the early afternoon, if all went according to plan.

At long last, the day had come to put all the training into motion. Race day fell on an unseasonably cool day in mid-October when a cold front had pushed through the Sunshine State, dropping temperatures twenty degrees as we slept. The swim was a nightmare. White-capped waves spilled over our heads as we swam with all our might through waters that were much warmer than the air temperature. The wind churned the lake surface and I felt as if I was in a washing machine. It took some time for my screaming heart rate to settle down to get into a rhythm of stroke, stroke, breathe, stroke, stroke, breathe.

Once I became comfortable with the way I was moving across the angry lake surface, my mind relaxed a bit and I kept company with thoughts from a thousand directions. It got easier to relax the farther from shore I swam: Ahhh.... this feels nice. The water is warmer than the air. Never mind that you can't see your hand in front of your face because of the dark water color. Ouch! Did someone just elbow me? What was Ricky up to today with his girls? I feel great - who needs a wet suit? Ew, lake water tastes terrible. Ohhhh- that WAS an elbow. One more time buddy and you are going to get it back. I wish the sun would come out. Darn these whitecaps -- makes it hard to breathe. How does Ricky feel today? Again with the elbow? That's it buddy -- wham! Ok, now I feel better....and I bet I won't feel that elbow in my side again. How much further to go? What would I do with such a diagnosis? For more than an hour, the misplaced thoughts bounced around in my brain seemingly with the break of every wave across my face.

After more than an hour of fighting off the waves, I was on my bike with comfort and confidence for the hilly, 112-mile second leg of the event. Once settled into a different rhythm of pedal strokes and breathing, again thoughts of Ricky took over. What was it like to be so close to death? How could he take such a leap of faith when the world's solution for cancer is chemicals? How did Marta cope with this situation? How was Chloe dealing with her Dad's sickness in spite of being so young herself? How were their finances since he could not work and medical bills were mounting? Questions continued to swirl around during the next six hours in the saddle. For a long while, I felt as if I were still bobbing in the water, so the questions sloshed around too.

Pinned to the back of my jersey was a "Racing 4 Ricky" sign that I had made and laminated. Throughout the race, people would encourage me with shouts of "Do it for Ricky!", "All right! You go girl!", and "RIDE FOR RICKY!" It was amazing, that by doing something for someone else, I was the one encouraged.

Once the race was completed, I hung around at the finish line to talk with other competitors as we recounted our experiences of the day. A cycling friend inquired as to who this Ricky was, after seeing the sign on my back. I shared his story then small talk came up about the cross-country bike ride that I was in the early stages of planning. She said that she had a Bucket List goal to "to ride across America" and asked me: "What is on your Bucket List?"

My reply to her was something like this: "I don't have a Bucket List. I have a Live It List. I don't want to put off things until a doctor tells me how much time I have left to do it; I want to start on it now."

Ever since Rob Reiner's comedy, *The Bucket List*, exploded in theaters in 2007, people have been creating their own lists of things to do before they die. Morgan Freeman and Jack Nicholson gallivanted the globe taking in all the sights, experiences and thrills they could before the terminal diagnoses they received from their doctors would put an end to it all. This light-hearted, feel-good movie prompted millions of people worldwide to ponder what kind of things they wanted to accomplish before their time ran out. It was both thought-provoking and entertaining but left me a bit unsettled.

Pursuing a dream to honor someone else not only drives you further, it helps that person too. By dedicating the race to Ricky, he was encouraged and had something to look forward to as he fought his own battle. There was accountability on my end to train harder, to make him proud, to help take my mind off discomfort as I trained. A distraction was helpful because training for this particular event course was grueling. Not all who start the race complete it. Hours of riding the bike and doing laps in the pool during hot, summer conditions made training a bit challenging at times. But by dedicating the race to him, quitting was not an option. These thoughts occurred to me as I ached more than once. What if Ricky quit? What if he gave up? What he was dealing with was far worse than any training day that I faced. Doing something big with someone else in mind also kept my ego in check, because it really wasn't all about me.

Living It means more than going places and doing something you have always wanted to do. In order for me to truly Live It, I transformed my desires into an experience with a much deeper meaning. By honoring someone else with an athletic endeavor, for example, a corner is turned. It no longer becomes doing something just for self, but shares the focus with others who have a need of some kind. This idea was something that I stumbled onto quite by accident when a friend and I waited too late to register for the Disney World half marathon in 2007. We had run it in 2005 and 2006, and dressed up as Disney characters for fun. We waited too late to register for the 2007 race. The only way to get in was by registering to run with a charity team.

After reviewing the options, I selected to run and raise money for the NF Endurance Team of the Children's Tumor Foundation. I learned more about neurofibromatosis, which is a genetic condition that 1:3000 are born with. And as I got to know some of the families affected by it, I promised myself that I would always help others in events like this. While it was fun to dress up like Pocahontas and run with my friend, the experience took on a much deeper meaning when I put on the Endurance Team's neon yellow running jersey. The Live It idea began at that time, even though I had no name for it. I just knew it was right and good to help in ways that I could.

The AquaBike race in Ricky's honor was complete. It was time to think about other goals on the list. Included on it: cycling across the country, tackling the daunting nineteen-mile ascent to the top of Pike's Peak in Colorado by bike, and writing a book. Now that check marks were beginning to replace dashes beside dreams on a sheet of paper, it was time to start preparing for the other adventures that lay in wait. The following year, we planned a late summer trip to visit our son in Colorado so I arranged to borrow a bike while there and knock off the Pikes Peak goal.

Ricky Perez came to meet us at the end of the journey. (Photo: Bill Draper)

To this day, it remains incomplete because a

snowstorm closed the roads to the summit the day I made my attempt. I got to Mile Thirteen, at 12,000 feet, but no higher. I plan to make another attempt the next time we visit our son. I want to ride it in the honor of a cadet who lost his life in a ski accident that happened when he was with some of his Air Force Academy friends during the 2014 school year. I would like to carry a stone with his name written on it and from the Academy grounds, placing it with the rocks at the summit that overlooks where he spent his last months of his life.

Thankfully, I have not had the unsettling news from a physician giving me a timeline for living, but the realization occurred to me that we all are on the path to death. I do have a limited time on this earth. It could end tomorrow in an auto accident. A diagnosis could come next year. All I know is that I have today to Live It, so Live It I shall. Jack, the young, 18-year-old USAFA cadet was living his dream when he passed. He had signed his name on a blank check to serve our nation as an officer in the US Air Force. When I breathe my last breath, I hope and pray to be living out my dream of using my life to leave a mark on this world. I want to Live It by doing something I love doing and benefitting others along the way. This is not a novel concept; people have been doing charity events for many years now. What makes it different is that I hope to do it as a lifestyle, rather than a one-time event.

In the coming pages you will find real stories that came to life as our team traversed the country. Some will bring you to tears, and some might even inspire you to come up with your own dream. I invite you to come with me from coast to coast over mountains and deserts, beside beautiful lakes and forests and to meet ordinary people with extraordinary lives. You will hear stories from wounded veterans and those who support them. To read about the dreams of those we met along the way. Peek inside our epic trip where achy muscles cried out and hearts fluttered with excitement. Come Ride Across the USA with me and let yourself dream along the way.

Why not?

1

Inception of a Dream

"If my son can ride cross country with cancer then I can ride across America without it!"

These were the words adamantly declared by the bike shop sales lady who was not only helping me purchase my first road bike but also sharing a piece of her life with me. At the time I had no idea the impact this story would have on me but I did feel something magical occur within my spirit. It vaguely reminded me of the first time I felt my daughter's flutter of existence within my womb. What I felt was the inception of a dream within my heart. I, too, could ride my bike across America one day. As Pam Hunt told me her story she concluded by saying: "If I can do it, anybody can." That resonated deeply within me and a dream began to take root.

The year was 2006 and I had only recently begun to compete in super sprint triathlons where the bike portion was ten miles or less. What an absurd thought: Riding my bike from coast to coast? But still – it spoke to me and I thought I wanted to do it. Why was I compelled by this story? Whatever made me think that I could do such a thing? It could be that I felt challenged by her. It could have been a delusion. What a crazy notion; I dismissed it after chewing on it for the fifteen-minute drive home.

As I recall Pam's story, her son rode from Portland, Oregon to Portland, Maine with a friend one summer. He didn't feel very well during the trip but chalked it up to the stress he was putting his body through. A month following the completion of his ride he went to the doctor only to discover that he had cancer. He received treatments and is cancer-free today but his initial diagnosis inspired his mother to dust off an old bike and begin riding to train for her own cross-country trek to raise money for a cancer research foundation. This was around 2004 and, as only a passionate Momma could, she began telling everyone what she was doing. A road bike was given to her, she planned her course and set out to ride it. She raised so much money for a national cancer charity that she even rode with Lance for a little while as a result of her fundraising efforts. With three months of pedaling, this fifty-five-plus-year-old mother completed her cross-country ride from San Diego to Cocoa Beach. Indeed, if she could do it, I could too ... one day.

My friendship with Pam developed over time as she took me out to show me how to ride a $600 aluminum frame road bike. She led me to the local hills and taught me how to shift gears and climb. She invited me to Ladies' Night at the bike shop so I could learn how to change a flat tire. I was so new to cycling that I heard that a carbon fork was a big deal but did not understand why. So new to this sport that one of her co-workers sold me a pair of cycling shorts and whispered to me, as he blushed, " Um, you are not supposed to wear underwear with these shorts." I even called them "pants" for the longest time and have friends to this day who remind me of their first rides with me.

One person in particular told his wife, "She's nice, but I just don't see any potential with her on the bike." Rookie that I was, I would sometimes ride in my workout spandex capris (not even cycling shorts), and I almost died of embarrassment one day when I returned from my ride only to find out that my black exercise pants with a thin blue line down the side were see-through when I bent over the handlebars in cycling position. No wonder the passenger of a truck at a red light yelled something about the color of my underwear. I had no idea. From that day forward I sported my one pair of cycling shorts, even if still damp from the wash until I could afford to buy more.

    A couple of years passed. Some annoying injuries from running helped me take a second look at cycling more seriously. By that time, the longest ride I had completed was a metric century with a triathlon club where I felt beaten up at the end because of poor mechanics and position in the saddle. It didn't really matter to me, however, because I was starting to really enjoy riding. The soreness in my seat and elbows paled in comparison with how running made this forty-something year old body feel.

    Occasionally Pam's words would make their way to the forefront of my mind and I would think "What if?" Then I would quickly dismiss the thought that I, a middle-aged mother who had so much to learn about cycling, would ever complete a trip across the country on two wheels. I bought the road bike so that I could fare better in local sprint triathlons. In those days I was in decent condition but had not ever worried about my nutrition very much. I had a little layer of fat that I carried with me everywhere I went. Another year or two later, I had to quit running altogether and began group cycling several days a week.

    I lost about fourteen pounds of squish practically overnight. I began eating healthier so that I could ride stronger and faster. Some people "ride to eat" but I discovered it worked better to "eat to ride." That is, to make sure that what I was eating was going to help me fuel properly for the next time out on the bike. As others in the club started to take note of my improvement, the dream of the Big Ride came back into play. With confidence building, I had mounting evidence to support the dream a bit better. I kept it to myself, though, because I didn't want my new-found cycling friends to think that I was crazy. I began to hear stories of others who knew someone who did the trans-America ride. I began to believe that I could – and would.

    I kept in touch with Pam and we never talked about a cross-country ride until four years later, when I told her that she had inspired me to do one of my own. She was supportive and excited, encouraging me all the way. She was a terrific resource to go to, so much so that I invited her to join us. Pam and I had numerous meetings, phone calls and email exchanges with me picking her brain during the planning phases of the Ride.

Rather than letting all of the "what ifs" and "I cannots" obscure my dream, I actually began to believe that it could happen. Every step I took in pulling this slightly insane dream off further built my belief that I could do it. Someone asked me, "Was there ever a day that you wondered if you could do it?" Without a blinking an eye my strong reply was, "No not once did it ever occur to me that I would fail."

> *"Going after a dream has a price. It may mean abandoning our habits, it may make us go through hardships or it may lead us to disappointment. But however costly it may be, it is never as high as the price paid by people who didn't live."* (Paulo Coelho)

Fulfillment of a dream must go hand in hand with the belief that it can be brought to fruition. The voice inside our heads that speaks the loudest is the one we will follow. The voice in my mind said without a doubt, "Tracy, you've got this" and I fully embraced it, never looking back. Perhaps therein lies the difference of an unfulfilled desire and the achievement of an aspiration.

Were there difficulties? Oh yes. Disappointments? Without a doubt. Times of hesitation? Certainly. But a time of doubting that I would ride my bike the length of the United States? Never. Not once.

The same belief that propelled me over 3,058 miles of deserts, mountains, monsoonal rain, temperatures over 120 degrees and across ten states also drives me to write this. While not having the same level of confidence in my writing as I have in my riding, I believe there are many readers who long to dream but then just leave it at that -- a far-fetched notion of "what it could be like, if only ... "

It is my hope to inspire people to conceive their dreams and then put feet on them.

2

Teeny Tiny Tri

*"Accept the challenges so that you can feel the
exhilaration of victory."* (George S. Patton)

Envisioning a transcontinental cycling trip at the very
moment when I purchased my first road bike wasn't the first
time I conjured up a new dream with just the slightest
provocation.

A few years back I had reached the point in my life
when our children were getting older and had their own
interests. Their ages ranged from nine to fifteen and I found
some free time in my schedule while they were at school. I
began to develop some interests of my own, as I only worked
part-time. One child was being a stinker, causing me a great
deal of stress. I had started running half marathons for a
charity and it was great because it gave me some time to work
through some problems and help others at the same time. It
was a win-win situation. Time passed and the children did
what kids do naturally -- they kept growing up and getting
more busy with school, sports and activities. What happened
to the problem child? Over time there was resolution and our
relationship is very close. Time and maturity are good healers.

Once our children began leaving home to explore
their own interests, I realized that I did not want to become
one of those mothers who fell apart when her kids moved out.
I needed to find something that I could pour energy into and
feel successful with. At church one day, the guest pastor began

his sermon telling us about his family, in particular his wife. He boasted about how she did a triathlon at Disney World: "If she can do it, anybody can." That piqued my interest. That sounded like something I could do too. I began "really running" (my prior skills were more like shuffling), trying to improve my time through interval training and sprints. TriNewbies.com became a resource for training and inspiration for me. I dusted off my old Target mountain bike that weighed more than thirty pounds and began riding it around my block. I paddled around in the lake nearby and decided to call that "swimming." Finally, I worked up enough nerve to do what I dubbed a "Teeny Tiny Tracy Triathlon" in our neighborhood. I timed myself and cheered myself on. Nobody knew about this until it was over because I was too embarrassed to be proud of it until I had seen it through.

It began with a six-minute circle swim in four feet of water (you know in Florida we have gators in our lakes). I swam as hard and as fast as I could in a twenty-foot radius then dashed to shore, put on my tennis shoes, shorts and tank top, then scampered across the two-hundred-foot park to the main road. From there I rode a 1.1-mile-loop three whole times as fast as I could. After the ride, I leaned my bike against the fence post and ran around the loop once. I finished the lap and crossed the imaginary finish line to the screams of thousands of pretend people lining the invisible chute. I threw my arms up in victory and promptly fell to the ground in disbelief that I could actually do a triathlon, even if it was just a Teeny Tiny one. I did it and I felt like a million bucks. It was time to dream again.

The fact that I could once again be an athlete was amazing to me. I was a mom for crying out loud – could I compete once more? Twenty-plus years had passed since high school. Who? Me? An athlete once again? Seriously? Oh yes.

Suddenly the work ethic of training hard that I learned in gymnastics as a youth returned and I was doing two-a-day workouts before I knew it. I began competing in triathlons and doing pretty well. My enthusiasm was hard to contain and soon I started having shooting pains in my hip and down my leg. The pain was so sharp and debilitating that my right leg would go out from under me at times. I went to the doctor and he looked at me and said, "How old do you feel?"

I sat a little taller and replied, "Twenty-four, Sir."

He then said with a smirk, "And how old are you really?"

I boldly and proudly announced, "Forty-two, Doctor."

His face got serious and he spouted, "You are *not* twenty-four and you had better train to *complete*, not to compete." (italics mine, emphasis his)

His comment ticked me off. Little did he know what he kindled in me. I love a challenge. If someone tells me I can't do something, watch out. I will show myself, and them, that I can and that I *will*.

I work hard and expect much. I presume others, including my family members, my clients, my teammates, to do the same. When my children were little Dr. James Dobson was my "go to source" for how to raise them. I read his books, listened to his radio show every day and took in everything he said. He advised that children will live up to what you expect of them and to expect a lot. I practiced that philosophy with them and I trust that they will indeed rise to the occasion. They are already proving themselves and it is wonderful to witness.

So, why not do the same for myself? Set a high bar and do what it takes to reach it. Being a mother didn't mean that my own life was over. It was time to set new goals and prove to myself that the athlete from my teen years, when I competed at a national level in gymnastics, was still alive within.

Perhaps I need to give the doctor a little credit because once my hip and leg pain subsided, I found myself again doing intense training sessions for sprint triathlons. It was then that other nagging injuries began to develop. I took a season off training and modified my regimen to include less time running. If I trained smarter not just harder, perhaps I could be competitive. This philosophy paid off: I won several races and it felt great to see my new training strategy net positive benefits.

As with most things in life, there are highs and lows. In 2009, while goofing around atop a thirty-foot-tall snow pile on the summit of Pikes Peak, I fell and ruptured a disk in my lower back. All I knew was that it hurt worse than natural childbirth and that I had a triathlon in three weeks so I had better suck it up. Stretching helped some but, after two months, I finally went to a physician in a reputable orthopedic clinic who showed me the MRI results.

He asked me, "How active do you want to be in your sixties?"

With determination I said, "Very."

His recommendation was, "Well, then maybe you should stop running now."

This was music to my ears since running was a difficult discipline that I did not care for and I felt as if I had received a pass from ever having to endure it again. Even in the midst of hearing that there were some serious issues with my spine, I was elated that I was permanently excused from running. The only reason for me to break out into a run nowadays is if something is chasing me.

Competition for me now meant AquaBike events, which are triathlons without the running portion. Starting out with shorter distances of 400 meter swim and 12 mile bike segments, I worked my way to an Olympic distance of 1500 meter swim and 22 miles of cycling. I did quite well in them. Cycling became my focus in 2010. I joined a local bike club and learned that road cycling was much more difficult than triathlon cycling because of the many safety rules to abide by when riding with a group. A new monster was growing within me and I just knew that I loved it. I could not get enough time on the bike and the training began paying off. The social aspect of group riding was incredibly fun. As I got stronger, some cycling friends encouraged me to explore the sport of racing.

Within the year I began road racing, which I didn't particularly enjoy. Racing a group of women on the bike wasn't quite as fun as long group rides for social reasons. Soon, the thought of doing something more fulfilling, such as riding from coast to coast, resurfaced again. The words of the my friend Pam began to filter through my thought process: "If I can ride across America on my bike, anybody can." The more I thought of it, the more I wanted to do it. Could I possibly, really ride from sea to shining sea? Questions swirled around in my mind. How does one train for that? How much does it cost? Are there transcontinental group rides to go on?

The dream was rekindled, thanks to a ruptured disc in my back.

The research began and very quickly I discovered that there are quite a few touring groups that do transcontinental rides. However, they were expensive with prices upwards of $8,000 and took up to eight weeks. Perhaps I could be a part of the Race Across America relay charity team that I knew a little about. However, after giving it some thought, *racing* across the country in a week didn't have much of an appeal to me. I also knew that I wanted to ride every single mile of the way, not just to be a part of a relay team. I felt as if I had one shot to make it all that I longed for. I wanted to see America but I could not take more than a few weeks away from my personal training clientele.

I finally realized a truth my Dad had taught me: "If it's going to be done right you have to do it yourself." I was going to plan my own cross country bike ride.

3

NO!

*"NO. ABSOLUTELY NOT. My wife will not be riding her
bike across the country! What – are you crazy?!"*

This was my husband's initial response the first time I
mentioned to him my desire to ride across the country in the
summer of 2012. After being married to him for eight years, I
knew he was capable of having such a reaction. So I brought it
up in a rather nonchalant manner – kind of testing the waters,
if you will. Now, mind you, I am a strong-willed individual
and having someone tell me that I can't do something doesn't
go over well. If you factor in my Southern Baptist roots,
however, I do have a deep level of respect for my husband as
head of the household and my ultimate protector. At times this
paradox breeds discontent within me and I struggle when my
man crosses my will. I force myself not to get uptight and
listen to him. It takes him no time to reiterate his point of
view: "There is no way you are going to do this. How can I
protect you when you are out there 'somewhere' riding your
bike in the middle of nowhere?!" I decide to take in his
concerns and not say another word about it... not yet anyway.
He has a good point but he has not heard me out at all. Later,
Tracy. Wait and let him chew on it.

As is often the result of being considerate of my man,
God gave me a sense of peace in my heart. If Billy did not

support this idea, there was no way I could pull it off or even begin to try. How could I be defiant with this man who loves me so much and truly cares more about my well being than anyone on earth? If this ride is meant to be, then it will be. If not, I will just have to find another dream to pursue.

I began questioning my motives for wanting to pull off this type of adventure. Pam, the sales lady from the bike shop, had lit a fire within me but what did I really hope to accomplish? I didn't have a dramatic impetus like she did because I didn't have a family member who had received a cancer diagnosis. The compelling desire was that it was a dream: It came out of left field and had a little bit of sense to it, a whole lot of unanswered questions, and the power to draw me in. It was the ultimate challenge on a bicycle. Many want to do it but only a handful of cyclists ever get to. There was the factor of the unknown, the adventure and the danger of such a ride that mystified me. Having thought about it for a few years (2006-2012), the flame grew bigger until I felt as if it was now or never. Pam did it in her fifties, but I wanted to fulfill this dream before I hit the half-century mark in my life. I began contemplating dreams. I knew what a dream man was – and I found him and married him. I knew what my dream house was – and I am currently living in it (that's another story in and of itself). I had the dream career of helping people understand the importance of both being fit and living a healthy lifestyle and then pointing them in that direction. But a dream bike ride?

Why not?

It would be easy to find more reasons *not* to follow the dream than to follow it. So I began listing all of the pros of following the dream.

Months later, I woke up and went about my routine of having a cup of coffee and checking in with the World (also known as Facebook). There are so many who use social media to communicate they are sad, lonely, broke, depressed or mad at the world. I try to use it to inspire and encourage others who may need a boost. This particular morning was no different and, as I sat to ponder what to type, these words found themselves coming to life from the keyboard and onto the screen:

> Dare to dream
> Research the steps to make it happen
> Count the costs
> Why not?

As I occasionally do, I shared this particular post with Billy via email but I had no idea the impact it would have on him. He replied to me that it spoke deeply to his heart and that he printed these words off and put them on his monitor at work. It hit home with him and really made him think of what dreams he had -- or didn't. Other than paying off our house, he really had not let himself dream, until now. He began talking about a dream car, how we could afford it, what kind of car it would be (a Mustang GT, of course). And we began doing the math. He attempted to talk himself out of buying the car a few times and would go over all of the reasons why he "shouldn't have his dream car" and then I reminded him that there was nothing wrong with it. We followed the formula above and, about two months later, he became the proud owner of his very own muscle car. It was so much fun to watch him drive it home with such a sense of pride. It made my heart happy to see him enjoy his dream.

Were the words I emailed to him an attempt to influence him so that I could do what I wanted? Not at all. The months that passed after my suggestion of a cross country ride gave me lots of time to ponder his reaction. After the amount of loss he has experienced in his life, how could I expect him to embrace a dream that involved such risks for me? Like many of us, my man needs time to contemplate big decisions. He rarely does anything impulsive, unless it has to do with sports. What I was attempting to do in those short phrases was to help him think of what kinds of dreams he had.

Not long after that, however, he came to me and said something like this: "Baby, if riding your bike across America is your dream, let's do it. If I can have my dream, you can have yours too." I was in shock. I had not talked about it once since he let me know of his initial disapproval of the idea. Of course, I was elated, but I needed to understand why he reacted so strongly in the beginning; so I inquired. This was his reply: He was afraid for my safety and he knows me so very well that if he hadn't over-reacted that I just might have taken off and done it anyway.

I guess all of that teaching in Sunday school about keeping quiet and letting God do the work paid off. Had I pushed the idea on him it would have had the opposite result. Had I tried to manipulate him, that would have been wrong and he would have figured it out anyway. Sometimes when life presents a boulder in our paths, we need not to try and shove it but instead quietly walk away.

Before too long we sat on the front porch in our rocking chairs with cups of coffee and started discussing this "big ride" in general terms. Here are some of the questions we discussed and our answers:

1. How much would something like this cost? Research presented a number between $30,000-$50,000. Ouch.
2. Who would pay for this? Each rider would pay their own way, unless sponsors would participate.
3. Who would go with me? I would not do this ride alone but have Billy along with me as many days as possible (he has a nice vacation package but not that nice).
4. What about other riders? A core group of five to seven other cyclists would be a nice group to go the entire journey with me.
5. Would this be self-supported or SAG [Support and Gear]?

We needed a SAG vehicle.

6. How long should this take? Five weeks is about all I can take off work.

7. What will the route be like? West Coast to East Coast.

We will have built-in rest days and be sure to get a good night's sleep either in an RV, homes, churches or hotels along the way. We would find a charity that we could put our full support into and help out others as we rode.

The preliminary judgment of "NO!" was coming undone with communication and mutual respect. Bill confessed that my question of "why not," in relation to a dream, really hit him hard. Why couldn't his wife ride three thousand miles? She has the strength and determination to pull off such a feat so it was time to think it through, do the research and count the costs. How could he stand in the way of his bride's dream? He could not – and would not. Billy became my biggest advocate, right–hand planner and best supporter. The "why not" question became the impetus behind the growing plan.

As I began to design a route from California to Florida, Billy looked for available domains for our website. He tinkered with all sorts of names and combinations of the words "ride, cycle, America, USA, United States, etc." While he worked for hours building our website, the dream took on feet of its own and began to walk with us every day. Most of our time after dinner was consumed with the plan. Oh, what fun this was -- to formulate such a plan with the love of my life.

From there we invested countless hours finding the right template, content, photos and such to build a site that would give us credibility and a professional look. Once it began coming together, it was time to begin looking for others to join me in the dream.

It took several months to compile a team of others that would meet the following criteria:

- Strong physically
- Strong mentally
- Able to take five weeks, or more, off work
- Financially able to contribute to team expenses
- Safe cyclists with years of experience
- Personality that could blend well with others under stressful conditions
- Willing to fundraise (not a requirement)

During all of this preliminary planning, somehow I came across a scripture in Lamentations that my inner spirit understood needed to be foundational for this ride. How did I know it was important and specifically for me? Think about it. Who reads Lamentations? According to the Merriam-Webster Dictionary, the very title of that ancient book in the Old Testament reads: "lam·en·ta·tion: an expression of great sorrow or deep sadness."

How could I possibly get much-needed encouragement or direction out of that kind of book? Was this a foretelling of how the ride would end? Would I regret doing this somehow? Only time would tell why it became my verse for this ride:

"Who can speak and have it happen if the Lord has not decreed it?" (Lam. 3:37)

On a sidenote, here is a little secret: The author of this book has a very strong will. Perhaps you surmised that truth already. Depending on how the will is wielded, it can be a blessing or a curse. I have used my will both for selfish desires and for helping others. This will has helped me to get through some tough circumstances in life but has also gotten me into trouble repeatedly. There is something about this particular verse that told me that no matter what I want, if

God's blessing is not on this event, no amount of my will was going to bring it about. There are just too many moving parts to this puzzle that were totally out of my control. It was a sobering thought and kept the planner on track by having to ask for Divine direction in every aspect of this endeavor.

The original sticky note with these words scratched on it in brown ink is still taped to my monitor today. It keeps me focused on Who is behind the planning and gets me back on track when my will tries to take over. And let me tell you, it happens a lot. One can usually tell when Tracy is in charge of her reaction, responses or behavior because it can become messy. This happened on several stress-filled occasions during our five-week ride.

"If you don't know where you are going, you'll end up someplace else." (Yogi Berra)

4

The Reason Why

"There are those who look at things the way they are, and ask why...I dream of things that never were, and ask why not?" (Robert Kennedy)

After toying for a few weeks with the idea of pulling off this wild dream, it was time to get serious about it or to chalk it up to a good idea that was just too hard to accomplish. I called a friend who has done RAAM (Race Across America) twice as part of a charity team to ask his advice. He wisely told me that the hardest part was deciding to do it. Once the decision was made, it was full steam ahead. He was right on.

Taking the next step meant doing some real planning. While this was my dream, I liked the idea of having someone else benefit financially from it. I have done many sporting events where Tracy was the only one who benefitted. They were each to satisfy my goals and for my glory. Something changed in me when I worked with a charity that helped children with a genetic disorder. We put on running events to raise money for a research foundation to find a cure. I learned how benefitting someone else through a personal goal was a win-win situation. The first step to making this dream come true was choosing a charity. There were so many worthy organizations from which to choose that this could take a while.

Camp Boggy Creek was one of my favorite

nonprofits and quickly became a frontrunner. It is a local camp for children in Florida who are chronically and/or terminally ill. For two years I had participated in their fundraising rides and had come to love its mission of enriching the lives of children with serious illnesses and also their families. Founded by Paul Newman and Norman Schwartzkopf, there are sister camps in various parts of the United States.

One day I had invited a few other cyclists for a tour of the camp, which is based in Eustis, Florida. It happened to be "Olympic Week" and the daily activities were related to Olympic sports. Since my friends and I had ridden our bikes to camp, we were clad in cleated shoes, spandex kits and helmets. We were able to visit one of the girls' cabins and talk with them for a few minutes. I noticed a pre-teen sitting at the table coloring by herself. Her smooth, hairless head gave me a clue as to what her condition might be. The girl with caramel-color skin did not look up at me as I sat next to her and began coloring. She simply said, "Do you know Lance Armstrong?" I replied in a soft voice, "Not very well." Her next statement was rather nonchalant: "I heard that he was pretty good at racing on bikes." The conversation continued, "Yes, he was. And they were big races." I went on to explain the best way I could what the Tour de France was like in a way that a youth could appreciate. Then I said, "And the best part was that he did it after cancer!" She froze for about two seconds, stopped coloring, then looked up at me with sunken ebony eyes and exclaimed, "*AFTER CANCER?*" Getting teary, I could only whisper "yes" with a broken voice. The relief that came over that child's face was priceless. She had found a reason to have hope. We colored in silence for a few more minutes. As I told her "bye" and looked at her, she had a peaceful smile across her face.

Originally, I chose to ride for Camp Boggy Creek and found two sister camps to plan the route around: one just north of Los Angeles and the other in Colorado. It was just a few months into planning when I realized to make a bigger impact and have more support, I needed to choose another quality charity that had a national focus. My contact at the Camp Boggy Creek agreed. By then the main route was already established: we would begin in Malibu, California and go through Colorado for a change in scenery. Despite the change in charities, the route would remain the same.

Another idea that came to me: With my family's military background, the next obvious choice to me was something to help our injured veterans. I began researching their needs and support systems. During the research process I came across a fact that was shocking to me.

> *"In 2010, an average of twenty-two service members a day committed suicide..."*

These words pierced my heart the first time I read them. Even today they affect me deeply. This sentence came from an article in *The Washington Post* and it described how our service members, for many reasons, are taking their lives by the thousands every year. At the time I came across this piece, I was deep in the throes of researching various nonprofit organizations that were dedicated to meeting the needs of our wounded service members. There are so many from which to chose and I wanted to be certain that I selected one that was reputable, honorable and actually gave the most money to those who needed it.

Twenty two lives each day gone; 680 a month eliminated; 8,084 lives taken by self in one year. And the death toll doesn't stop. These numbers represent far more lives lost in 2010 (and years since) than those lost during the combined years of war in Iraq and Afghanistan. These American warriors surely battled a much bigger force from within than from the enemy on the outside.

What causes a person to take his own life? Having

never been in so much as a fist fight, I cannot fathom what the violence of war may be like. My family life was very safe, secure and stable while growing up as an Army brat. My father was an officer and retired as a lieutenant colonel from the Army in 1982. He saw combat in Vietnam when I was a toddler. As I grew up I knew that he was a Ranger, Green Beret and Airborne but had no real appreciation for what that meant, except that he was an officer and that he was important to the Army and it was important to him.

He was an excellent father, providing well for us, making sure that we were in a good school and neighborhood, teaching us to be independent, and sacrificing career advancement opportunities for the family (I found out much later on). He was happy, energetic, well-liked and seemed to be unscathed by what he lived through during the war. Not very desirous about talking much about his experiences in Vietnam, he had two or three stories that he would tell and that was enough. A younger, more dramatic Tracy tried to believe that he must have been scarred deeply by combat and that he just buried his feelings (yes, I watched too much pop-psychology on television). Such was not the case at all with my Dad.

But now as I have learned more about human behavior and life itself, I can see that it is possible to live through terrible situations and be able to cope with it, process it and move on. Can you imagine how difficult it would be to hold on to a dream while fighting destructive forces on many fronts? My Dad had the ability to persevere during the horrors of war and put it behind him. One valuable lesson he has taught me as I reached adulthood: "What has happened is behind us. It's time to move forward." This is a rich, hard truth and is very difficult for some to uphold. There are some who can press on through whatever difficulties of war or life in general present them.

Not everyone can move ahead so easily. Could it be

that today's fabric of society is woven together much more loosely than when Dad was brought up? A stable family is hard to come by. Many, if not most of us, have already had at least two very hard knocks in life and it is my belief that some may be one traumatic event away from the main cause of suicide: hopelessness.

Hopelessness does not come overnight. It takes time to develop; it begins with feelings of helplessness. To feel as if one has no control in some area of a person's life is where it all begins. To be without hope, whether real or imagined, is a dangerous place to be. I have been there a time or two, so I write this carefully from personal experience, conviction and passion. The dark feelings of despair can become reality for someone who has undergone traumatic experiences.

> *"Hope deferred makes the heart sick but a longing fulfilled is a tree of life."* (Proverbs 13: 12)

I won't go into detail of my bouts with helplessness. Suffice it to say that once the downward spiral of negative thinking and consequential destructive behavior begins, it is difficult to stop. But it is possible. Help is needed from the outside because there is little to no belief from within that circumstances can be remedied. Just as stated so wisely in that favorite Proverb, sickness comes from hope that is dashed. When one gives up on his situation then, over time, illnesses of the mind and the body can enter the picture.

As I combed through dozens of charitable organizations, the very name Hope For The Warriors instantly grabbed me. HOPE. Ah yes: *the antidote to suicide.* I was enthralled with their mission statement to assist post-9/11 service members, veterans and their families. The fact that Hope sets out to treat the root of the problem, injured veterans and their families re-integrating into society, and offers them solutions spoke loudly to me. With so many who feel hopeless, Hope restores a sense of self, family and future. I wanted to partner with an organization that provides hope to the hurting.

It sounded like a perfect choice but needed further investigation.

After researching the group on Charity Navigator, a national rating system for nonprofits, the initial feelings I had about Hope For The Warriors were confirmed. I decided it was worth a phone call to learn even more about them. After several conversations with their team director, I knew I was on to something good. The timing of this was about a year prior to the ride itself, so we agreed to keep in touch and build our partnership as time drew closer for the ride.

Why was this so important to me? Because I knew that if I was asking people to donate to a cause, I had to believe in it 100 percent. The more I learned about the Hope group, the more I appreciated what they do and how they make a genuine impact on the lives of thousands of armed services members and their families. H4W is a grassroots effort that started in 2006 by two wives of Marines. They saw a need in the lives of wounded soldiers and sought to meet it. Robin Kelleher and Shannon Maxwell founded H4W back in 2006 after seeing many needs of our injured Marines returning to Camp Lejeune.

Robin is the President of Hope. She tells the story of her husband's deployment to Iraq in 2003, when she was pregnant and "unsure of how our lives would change so dramatically over the next few years." Helping care for the families of men and women serving with her husband was just the start. Eighteen months later, a family friend serving in Iraq was hit by a mortar round. His wife flew to Germany, where he had been transported. The couple returned to Maryland "to begin the long recovery journey and what would be the beginning of Hope."

The Marine wife marshaled help from Shannon to

serve the growing group of wounded soldiers. Both runners, the two planned the inaugural Run For The Warriors. With complete support from the leaders of Camp Lejeune, the run drew two thousand runners who showed their support in the pouring rain on May 19, 2006.

Faced with such support and the strength of military wives, the women quickly grasped that they had embarked on a larger mission. Robin writes: "Doing more than just a run was not a choice for us. It was clearly what we were being asked to do."

These women believe that hope isn't ambiguous and that it is "a solid foundation and the greatest of gifts." It is also their inspiration. Knowing the struggles of military wives, the Hope group awarded scholarships to them initially. Now, a decade after the group formed, it has served members of the military and their families in every state.

> *"This family has grown in the rich stories of grace and pain, of sorrow and joy and of desperation and hope. My personal journey has taught me that giving up is not an option and that if you wait patiently, hope will show you what comes next."* (Robin Kelleher)

To partner with Hope was an easy choice for me because of my love for the military and the fact that it has played such a big role in my own life. To be able to help provide hope and restoration for our most deserving is an honor. We have a son who will soon receive his commission in the Air Force as a second lieutenant. In a new age of war on terror, the need to support our military weighs heavily on me. Hopefully our son will never need to enlist the services offered by Hope, but it is reassuring to know that Hope is there for those who need it.

Finally, the dream was beginning to take shape. It

took a good eight months to invite others to join the team, and we still had a spot or two open. Each cyclist selected was someone that I knew in one way or another from cycling groups in central Florida. I felt pretty good about those who had agreed to the mission. You will get to know each team member as the chapters unfold. We had a driver volunteer to support us.

A client of mine offered the use of his trailer to haul our supplies. A charity had been selected; the route was almost complete. A cycling fundraiser to support Hope For The Warriors was planned for Veterans Day weekend 2013.

Excitement within the cycling community was mounting as more people heard of our adventure. With eight months to go until the ride's start, there was still much to be done. Would we get corporate sponsors? What kind of lodging would we have each night? How would we all get along? These questions and more had yet to be answered.

5

The Countdown

"Without leaps of imagination, or dreaming, we lose the excitement of possibilities. Dreaming, after all, is a form of planning." (Gloria Steinem)

"284 days until the ride starts!" the email to the team proclaimed. That seemed so long to wait, like a woman who just got word that she is expecting a baby. Nine long months. A part of me feared that it might fly by due to the amount of work that still needed to be accomplished. The mission remained in the forefront of my mind. Day and night I was consumed with planning and organizing this dream.

Since some people invited to join the team were unable to participate for various reasons, it took a few months to find others who were a perfect fit for the group. I tried to match personalities and select a good team that would work together well. We would have to share close quarters and endure many frustrations. It was extremely important to get the best mix of age, speed, strength, skills, and personality type for this adventure. This was not an easy task in the least. Ideally, I wanted eight cyclists and one driver. But we ended up with seven riders and one driver who wanted to ride as much as he could. For the most part, his desire to ride with us was OK. After all, he was along to support the team and it would be good for him to get in some exercise and ride with us.

The downside of having our driver with us was that it would present some logistical issues. For example, Clay would have to leave the SAG parked from where we stayed overnight and ride part way with us, then return to it by himself. What if he had a mechanical issue - or worse -- a crash? No one would be with him to help him; we would all be going towards our next destination. His primary role was to drive for us and support the team; riding was secondary. On the other hand, when we had a second SAG driver (Pam or BillyD), it was perfectly fine for him to get some riding in.

In the late spring of 2013, we had an exciting breakthrough. The Mount Dora Community Trust (thanks to Ed Brooks) offered to sponsor our training kits. Once our logo design was complete, the uniforms were designed and ordered. They arrived just in time for a fall fundraiser that we put on for Hope For The Warriors. We named it The Warrior Ride and raised over $3,400 as well as bucket loads of awareness and excitement in Central Florida. Most participants had never heard of the Hope group, so it was great to share with the riders our reasons for choosing to ride across the country for this organization. The ride was on Veterans Day weekend, and we felt it was a big success with 162 cyclists who came out to ride in 40- or 100-mile routes.

During the Christmas holidays, Hope For The Warriors Team Director Steve Barto was in Tampa on business. He made a quick trip to meet our team and sit in on our December planning meeting. He took notes and returned to his office in New York with a list of our desires, support needs and overall plan. Hope had a passenger van that we had asked to use for our SAG. We also requested marketing support, a banner flag to post at our rest stops and auto magnets with both our logos on them to let others know what we were doing as we traversed the nation.

We still had a few spots open on the team. A couple of members came on board initially but had to back out due to personal or financial reasons. That was unfortunate because I had selected each of these men because I knew they would make good additions. However, they each knew their situations the best so we had to trust their decisions.

In January 2014 our team began doing training rides together with an endurance cycling group known as Randonneurs. What is a Randonneur? The definition on their website states: "Randonneuring is long-distance unsupported endurance cycling. This style of riding is noncompetitive in nature, and self-sufficiency is paramount. When riders participate in randonneuring events, they are part of a long tradition that goes back to the beginning of the sport of cycling in France and Italy. Friendly camaraderie, not competition, is the hallmark of randonneuring." These endurance rides vary in distances from 100 kilometers (124 miles) to 1600 kilometers (994 miles). The "Superbowl" of Randonneuring is in Paris every few years where those who qualify ride 1600 km for honors. For training, our team had decided to do three rides with the Randonneurs: the 200-, 300- and 400-kilometer ventures (124, 187 and 252 miles respectively). We had one per month for the first three months of the new year.

The idea behind the training-ride series was multifaceted:

1. Get to know each other better. Who was even-tempered? Who had leadership skills? Was there a complainer in the mix? What were our sleeping habits like? Did some friendships need nurturing? Were there pet peeves that we could learn about each other?

2. Learn each other's riding styles. Could everyone hold a straight line while riding? Was everyone cautious? Did we all subscribe to the same safety rules? What was each team members' riding level? Were there any hot dogs on the team? Did anyone ride too aggressively? Every rider has a style and

it was better to learn that prior to the launch of this challenge.

3. Become comfortable riding on the wheel of each team member. With the warning of high winds that were sure to accompany us along the way, we needed to be able to draft from each other effectively to take turns conserving energy and then facing the wind head-on. Since we would certainly shift around in our pace line, it was important to me that we each knew what to expect from the person riding directly in front of us -- just inches between our wheels at times.

4. To bond as a team and to build base mileage. My hope was that we would develop deep friendships that would be long-lasting (yeah, I know; that is a girlie idea but I liked it anyway). Since we had so many miles to cover together, we needed to genuinely get along or else there could be big problems. Friends look out for friends. It's that simple. We needed to each have some real care and respect for each other. That takes time to develop.

We had a 200-kilometer ride, which was 122 miles, in January; a 300-kilometer ride for 187 miles in March; and a 400-kilometer of 252 miles during one day in April. The 400 kilometer was our best training ride. We started in the rain at 5 am and headed north towards Jacksonville, where we encountered severe thunderstorms and tornado watches. Our phones were tucked away in sealed bags in our pockets so we did not get the warnings of the dangerous weather conditions that lie ahead, but we knew they were harsh.

The temperature dropped into the upper fifties and by the time we stopped for lunch, we were drenched and cold but still getting along well. Temperatures did climb into the low seventies before the sun went down. We finished at 10:17 pm with no more rain. Tired, but thrilled to have done this together, we felt we were ready for whatever challenges lay ahead. We didn't expect to ever have to ride 252 miles in one day, but we now knew that we could – if we had no other choice.

This 400-kilometer ride was a tryout for our last added team member. He passed our test and would now go home to discuss joining the team with his wife. Within a few days, he called to say that he was "in." Our team was now set: Ruth, Marion, Keith, Scott, Ed and Bill were the riders. Clay was our full-time support driver and part-time rider for the entire trip; Pam provided us inspiration and intermittent support. My husband, BillyD, was the primo website builder, part-time driver, and Twitter manager.

Our team was now complete. Each person on the team brought something different to the mix. Team members:

Ruth is semi-retired, a strong, solid rider, pretty quiet and easy to get along with. I met her via FaceBook and when we met in person on a New Year's Day Ride in 2012, we became good friends.

Marion, a Netherlands native, is a nurse with both a contagious smile and a zeal for life. She came to some of my cycling workshops to get stronger and to learn how to climb better.

Keith is Ruth's boyfriend and they are the dynamic duo on bikes. An entrepreneur, he, too, is quiet and strong. I met Keith on my first 200K ride in 2012.

Scott is light-hearted, talkative and energetic. We met one year at the Mount Dora Bicycle Festival and I was impressed that he was doing a 100-mile ride on a mountain bike.

Ed is a retired fire chief and EMS. He is the first person I asked to join the team because we had ridden 167 miles in one day on the Cross Florida ride in 2013 and I thought he would be a good teammate.

Bill is a retired certified public accountant who also served in the Army as a member of special forces. He is focused but enjoys a good laugh. We met as members of the Florida Masters cycling club and did some riding together through that group. To avoid confusion, I refer to him as "Bill" and my husband as "BillyD."

Clay is in his 60's, retired from the Navy and very easy going. He had a career dealing with horses, so I knew he could drive a trailer. We also met through the Florida Masters club.

The plan was for us to fly together from Orlando to Los Angeles, with Scott departing from Jacksonville and meeting us at LAX airport. Clay and Dad would drive our SAG vehicle and trailer full of supplies to California a week ahead of time. Pam and her husband, John, would meet us at the end of Day One in Victorville, California. BillyD would meet us in Williams, Arizona, at the end of week one. He would stay with us until we got over the Rockies.

Amid all of the successful planning, however, a dose of reality came to me as a big surprise. With so many things going in the right direction, this particular morning ride dealt a number on me as it snuck up, out of nowhere, sideswiping me. The words below recount the mental battle that I faced and how it was resolved.

Moments of Doubt –April 2014

I knew this day would come but was honestly surprised by the timing of it. I believed doubts might come as we traversed the Rockies or suffered through big winds in the

Plains. But now? We still had six weeks before we even begin this journey.

Trying to keep in a realistic mindset of what lie before us, I had already adopted the term "DD" for such "Doubt Days." I believed that at least some of us would succumb to such mental warfare at some point. By coining a phrase, I had planned on sharing with the team that these days would come and, when they did, we could deal with the doubt easier by giving each other a pass and claiming a DD for ourselves.

But to wake up and have it greet me this morning, weeks prior to the ride, was unexpected. To make it worse, the weather outside was gloomy, damp, cool and just plain blah -- a perfect match for my mood. Forcing myself to get on the bike and take a ride despite my feelings, I convinced myself that a short ride would at least make me feel better.

Why was I feeling this way? Simple: I had heard some negativity of what a couple of naysayers had been spreading about.

"Yeah, riding 3,000 miles in 31 days - sure..."

"Doubtful that their bodies can take such a beating. 100 miles a day is going to take a toll. I wonder if everyone will make it?"

"I don't think they know what they're doing. Sure fail."

"Who does Tracy think she is?"

"Are they crazy?"

Isn't it interesting how others' words can bring us down? Whether they are dealing with skepticism, jealousy, or spite, some people seem to get joy out of trying to undermine the dreams and aspirations of others. It happens all too often and, while we may know better deep within, we allow someone else's doubt to become our own.

Arguing with myself the entire time I rode, I tried to force myself to believe that the endorphins were about to flow and my mood would suddenly and completely change. That didn't happen. Along this particular route, I almost always saw a cycling friend at his home on Lakeshore Drive. Sitting in his office, he overlooks the road and the lake as he works. I looked for him, seeing him in his usual posture at his computer with his lamp on and the top of his head peering over his monitor. I threw up a hand, flashed a big smile and waved like crazy. "No Ordinary Man," as we affectionately call him, did not even look up as I slowed to a crawl of 14 mph to pass his house. Waving my entire arm like a madwoman didn't even get his attention.

And so the battle ensued in brain and spirit. Conversations of past negative experiences with others crept into my mind and further stole my joy. What is wrong with me? Why do I feel like this? Deciding to end this emotion-filled ride, I followed the roundabout for a full 360 degrees and headed home. Surely things would be better there -- at least the voices would quit or my mood would change.

I came home in a defeated state, just thirty minutes later. My two normally happy-to-see-me dogs didn't even bother to get up and greet me. Now I knew that something was amiss in the universe. What was I to do with all of these overwhelming emotional feelings? First, discount it as the hormonal imbalance of a 48-year-old. Secondly, go deeper within and draw from what I know is true. I knew I could not let this pattern of negative thinking continue so I relied on what someone had taught me in the past: Recite what the truth of the matter is, not what I am feeling. Truth overrides emotion whereas feelings can change with the wind. I choose Truth.

Truth is that our team is about to do something BIG and benefit many people. Truth is that nothing is wrong with me; that others are negative for whatever reason and say things to make themselves feel better when people attempt to break out of a stereotyped mold (or something like that). Truth is that I am made well, loved deeply and that nothing is wrong with me, except the fact that I am merely a mortal. I make the same mistakes that so many others do; heck, I even make some unique ones at times. Truth is that there will be Doubt Days for me during our five-week feat. Truth says that I will also have Strong Days, Successful Days and days when I surprise even myself. Truth is that the wimpy little things I face (and try to make into big things in my mind) are really nothing compared with what our wounded warriors face day in and day out. If I think I have voices of doubt in my brain, can you imagine what they hear? Oh how my DDs are tiny in comparison. Pick up, Tracy, dust off and get on with your mission: Bring hope to the warriors. Ride on with a head held high.

That little pep talk did the trick. When faced with such thinking it is imperative that we turn it around or face the possibility of some serious consequences. Sometimes we can resolve the issue on our own with a pep talk; other times we may need the help of a friend's sounding board to help us sort out fact from fiction. When we make decisions based on emotion instead of fact, we often make mistakes. The unfortunate line of thinking from that morning ride proved to be good training for days that lie ahead that summer.

Back to business at hand, including counting down the events leading up to the day of departure. Because there were so many parts to this moving puzzle, intricate planning must occur. Big dreams often have big price tags. The bigger the dream, the more possibilities of failure. We had to keep in mind that "if it is worth doing, it is worth doing right."

To ensure the success of the project, we needed a backup plan in place: What if our SAG had mechanical problems? What if someone got sick - or worse yet - injured on the ride? The team worked well together through regular team meetings to address many of the unforeseen issues that could interrupt the plan. If the SAG broke down, we would continue to the next planned destination without it. Clay would handle the situation and get a rental if need be. We had no wiggle room in our schedule. If someone was injured, the team would continue. Depending on the seriousness of the injury, someone may stay with them. Some concerns would simply have to be dealt with as they arose.

On Memorial Day Weekend we hosted another fundraising Warrior Ride in north Orlando. It was a week before the team departed and was our "farewell" ride with our many friends. We got to debut our official team kits. I'd like to think we looked inspiring and professional.

This time, we told our supporters that all the funds donated would go to our emergency trust account and all money left in that account after the ride would be donated to Hope For The Warriors. Over 200 cycling friends came out to support our mission and wish us well.

As for the money collected on that day, we kept our word. Taking in around $6,000, it was nice to know that there was such a line in our budget for unforeseen emergencies. The main concern was that the SAG vehicle could have a problem, which can be very expensive to repair on the road. With such a tight schedule and zero room for varying from the daily itinerary if we encountered vehicle trouble, we would be forced to rent another one to stay on schedule. That can be quite costly.

Each team member contributed $3,000 to the same trust fund from which we would pay our expenses. Initially, I believed that sponsors would come on board and would help with advertising and that the original budget of $35,000 would be covered completely. This was not to be so. I was very surprised that more businesses did not support such a great cause and mission, and I grew weary of asking. It felt as if I were the only one on the team soliciting sponsors. Hearing "No" over and over was also a discouragement. Rejection is never easy to take.

Didn't these companies believe in us?

The economy was still struggling to make a comeback, which is the reason why most business owners said they could not support us. I found ways to trim our budget so we could meet what we were paying into it (a novel thought, huh?). So we now had seven cyclists giving $3,000, which gave us $21,000. Clay was told to donate a lesser portion since he was driving and supporting us the entire way. With our fundraising and some other donations that came in specifically for team expenses, we were going to cut our funding close but manage to be in the black -- as long as there were no big surprises.

Our largest line item was lodging. For months I made phone calls and sent dozens of emails asking for places to stay. Once most potential hosts learned who we were riding for, they opened up their doors for us free of charge. There were so many wonderful people who took us in, loved on us and did so with such willingness to serve our team and the wounded veterans for whom we were riding.

The second costliest part of the big ride was food. After asking a team member if he would help come up with an eating plan for the team he stated that we will just stop and have a meal where we could find it. It was not exactly what I had in mind for a plan, but it had to do. In randonneuring, there is no SAG. You carry your own food or plan to stop at convenience stores and restaurants along the route.

This is what he was used to, and since no one else seemed to be worried, we expected to figure it out on the road. Another team member had a friend who wanted to purchase our own special favorite nutrition for us ahead of time. That was a real blessing and we were all so appreciative. Being the planner that I am, I had to really trust that this would work out. There were only a few days of riding in isolated parts of the country. We would need stocks of food in the SAG and extra ice in the coolers.

Team member Ruth is a giver. She is loved for her contagious smile and big heart. We agreed to rent her brand new Nissan Pathfinder for the SAG vehicle. It was great to know we could count on this vehicle to get us through the journey. It was another huge piece of the puzzle that came out of nowhere. We had hoped a car dealership would provide a vehicle for us but none came through, despite many requests. As it turned out, it didn't matter. It may actually be nice not to have a sponsor to have to depend on. I had no time or energy to spend on the "why nots" that tried to take up residence in my brain. Press on. There comes a time when it is best to find other avenues to pursue when things don't turn out the way you hoped. The challenge is to know when that time arrives. I knew that it had come.

Another major expense was gasoline. Since our equipment was going to go west a week before us, I gave Clay gift cards for gas, food and lodging from our expense account. Dad met his expenses on the way to California, mostly for food, and the hotel was paid through Clay's travel budget so as not to hit our team account. We wanted every possible dollar to go to Hope For The Warriors.

Immediately after the Memorial Day Warrior Ride, we loaded the trailer and waved our goodbyes to Clay and our bikes. It was a little scary to see him disappear down the road. Was the feeling due to knowing that there was no turning back now? Was it because our bikes were out of our watchful eyes? I have to admit it was a little of both.

There were a couple of times during all of this planning that the thought occurred to me: "What on earth am I doing?" As quickly as it came into my mind, the thought vanished with anticipation. As for the safety of my prized golden-colored bike and all of our supplies, I just had to trust that the locks on the trailer would deter any potential thieves, and that there would be no mechanical trouble along the way. Our treasures were in good hands.

As Clay departed, Marion, Ruth and I looked at each other with teary eyes and hugged, knowing that the next we would be together would was in eight days at the Orlando International Airport. Scott was with us and had his usual boyish grin across his face. He, too, was excited and a little nervous.

That final week was full of last-minute planning, confirmation phone calls, outreach to the media, and a few interviews for local papers. It felt as if I was walking in a fog, checking off one list after another, saying "so long" to friends, clients and even my own family members.

At last the day had come to catch the flight to LA. On Monday, June 2, BillyD and our youngest child, Suzie, took me to the Orlando International Airport at 6:30 am. They left me at the curb in front of the terminal as the sun lifted higher in the sky. It was a humid morning, but cloudless. We had a bittersweet farewell that was cut short by a security guard, whose shrill whistle let BillyD know that he had to move the car. As I quickly walked to the terminal doors, I caught them both looking back at me as I turned for one last glance at them. It was somber with forced smiles. What were they thinking? Did they fear for my safety? What would life be like after the ride? Would I be a changed person? Would the dream be worth it? Would we have to reacquaint ourselves with each other? I have never been away from home or family this long. A fleeting and dramatic thought occurred to me: Was this the last time I would see them? Would tragedy befall? Only time would tell. I elected to dismiss that thought.

While I knew that they would worry about me, I continued to walk toward the check-in counter with resolve and excitement. For now, I had a plane to catch, a team to connect with and a mission to accomplish. My steps quickened as I made a beeline to the security area after the woman at the ticket counter wished me a good day. As I worked my way through security, I prayed for unity, patience, safety and most of all strength for us. I was the first one to arrive at the gate. This would be the last time for quite some time that I would get to be alone with my thoughts. It was a peaceful, quiet few moments from the curb to the terminal.

One by one, texts came in with a status update from team members. All of us sported our Ride Across USA T-shirts and huge grins as we saw more and more of us gather. We asked a Southwest Airlines employee to take our photo in front of the gate marked for Los Angeles. Some of us were giddy and some kept their calm, cool and collected faces on. But we all knew that everyone was excited -- and a little nervous.

Ed's wife is a flight attendant for Southwest. Because of her charm and the fact that all other attendants knew her, we received special attention on the plane. Bags of peanuts and crackers were put in our laps for later. Each attendant stopped by to visit and wish us well. Midway through the flight, an announcement came over the intercom that "some VIP guests are on the plane." A ninety second blurb about the Ride Across USA caught everyone's attention. At the end of it, the passengers broke out in applause and each of us let it sink in.

Before we knew it, it was time for us to descend into LAX. Another announcement came over the intercom and, again, more cheers. We passed out our Ride Across USA cards that the Hope group had made for us to distribute. Directions on the card asked people to go on social media and post that they had met us and spread the word of our mission. People were excited to follow us. Many asked questions as we disembarked the plane and others talked with us, asked for photos and cards while we all made our way to baggage claim. It was wonderful to see my Dad, who had just found Scott. Both were easy to pick out because of their Ride Across USA T-shirts and beaming smiles. Clay was waiting with the SAG in short-term parking.

Once all bags were accounted for, we piled into the

SAG and Dad's rental, and we headed to the Malibu beach house that had been arranged for us. Believe it or not, it was more cost effective to rent a three-bedroom home on the beach than rent five hotel rooms for two nights in Santa Monica. A beautiful day greeted us with temperatures in the mid-sixties, a cloudless sky and energy in the air. Malibu was spectacular! Crisp air, blue skies and abundant sunshine greeted us as soon as we got away from the bustle of Los Angeles. We drove right by the beach where we would launch our journey in about thirty six hours.

My heart raced and eyes filled with tears as I looked over the Pacific Ocean. Chills overtook my body and I felt a shiver. It was much more than the cool sixty degree temperatures that forced the goosebumps. Dad, Marion, Ed and I shared the ride with Dad as the others loaded up the Nissan. While heading to the beach house, a call came in from the editor of the *Orlando Sentinel*, who had been sharing lead up stories with the community. It was exciting to be able to report that we had indeed arrived. We were heading to the beach house and decided to stop for lunch. Another call from a reporter for the *San Fernando Valley Sun* was awaiting an interview. Tidbits of pressure eased onto my shoulders as I realized the dream was within reach. Oh my.

Upon arrival at the unassuming beach house, we each decided where the best sleeping spots were for us. We moved in, packing ten adults into a three-bedroom, two-bath house. Thankfully, there were lots of couches. Selflessly Scott, Ed and Bill each took a couch, rather than a bed. The men were gentlemen, allowing for the ladies to have the best accommodations. Since Clay and Dad had been rooming together from Alabama to California, they got the L-shaped bedroom with purple walls and two single beds. Scott mentioned that he would gladly blow up his air mattress on the back porch and be lulled to sleep by the ocean waves, gently lapping onto shore. It was refreshing to see the interaction and courtesy of the team members. I was a little nervous about being the leader of the group because of my upbringing, but I also knew that the team was all here at my invitation and that they expected leadership from me. In no way did I want to lord authority over the team, believing that we were all adults and that each had something to contribute. However, leadership was needed and it was up to me since this was my big idea.

The side of the house that faced the Pacific Coast Highway looked like a fortified military encampment. Perhaps this was the builder's idea to keep burglars from thinking there was anything nice inside. However, from the ocean side it boasted several six-foot diameter circular windows that framed the ocean as an artist would do on a mural painting. The waves crashed onto the shore some twenty feet from the back deck stairs. Rocks of varying sizes ducked under the high tide before the waves withdrew to the sea twice a day. As we settled in, the Goodyear blimp made a cameo appearance as it drifted north up the coast. Dolphins had been spotted playing in the surf as well. Despite this incredible scenery, we were all keenly aware of why we were here: We had a mission to complete.

The views were a bonus, very much appreciated, but could not be a distraction. Several of us were enjoying the views of the ocean but were beyond ready to put our bikes together and stretch our legs for a few miles. And that is just what we did. Five of us explored Malibu by bike for about ninety minutes, stopping for photos, climbing on over-sized reptile statues at a park and getting buzzed by California drivers. More and more states require drivers to stay three feet from cyclists. If this state had such a law, drivers seemed clueless about it.

It felt good to release some energy but we soon returned to the house to clean up for dinner.

A half mile walk after the post-ride showers took us

to a nice restaurant that overlooked the ocean at sunset. It was spectacular. Not all of our team members had been on the West Coast. When might we return? Each of us relished the beauty of the ocean and its rocky shore. The beaches of Florida have their own special qualities, but to realize that the waters before us had entirely different stories to tell was incredible. The rocky shorelines, different fauna, geology and overall scenery was as dreamy as the wonderment of what lie ahead. I gazed for many moments from the house and restaurant at dinner just staring, offering gratitude to the Creator of this amazing part of the world. Shortly after, with full bellies and bodies that had a full day, we ambled back south on Pacific Coast Highway and put ourselves to bed while the countdown clock continued to tick.

The next morning we had an easy bike ride planned to meet a local man I had met via email; he was going to show us some sights. His name was Scott and, to my pleasant surprise, he was a professional photographer. He was a delightful tour guide. We made an obligatory stop at the Santa Monica Pier and enjoyed that scene for a few minutes before pedaling slowly to Muscle Beach -- but found only one or two semi-buff guys strutting their stuff. Making the best of it, we took our own photos and hoisted our bikes overhead as if we were weightlifters.

I could not help but be overcome multiple times that we were actually *here*. Small talk faded on this little warm-up ride and I became increasingly aware of what was before us. It felt a little scary -- and so exciting -- at the same time. In my mind, thoughts oscillated between being in the moment of the beauty and being in the reality of what was about to occur. So many depended on us. So many supporters were counting on us. It was just about time to get this ride underway. The weight of a little more pressure found its way onto my shoulders.

After about 15 more miles into this touring ride, I decided to head back to the house as there were final details to settle before we would start in less than 19 hours. Bill went back with me so I didn't have to make the trip alone and I appreciated that. I was glad that he joined the team; I felt like he had a lot more experience than several other team members had and I liked that he was quiet. When he did speak, it was something worth listening to.

The rest of the team stayed with Tour Guide Scott and went further south for lunch, then ice cream. After the ride, via email, he asked if he could meet us at our launch the next morning to take photos. Of course I said "yes." We would now have professional pictures of our starting moments for personal keepsakes, our Facebook page and website. What a gift.

Time continued to tick away ... T-minus 15 hours. We decided to cook in house rather than dine out that night. This turned out to be fun because everyone pitched in as a big family, each with his or her own part to add to dinner. Dad and I went to the grocery store to purchase spaghetti and fixings. Three did the cooking; others did the cleanup. It was time to review the plan for the morning then head for bed. T-minus 10 hours now. Nerves attempted to take over but now was not the time to get tangled up in fretful thinking. The next thing I knew it was after 10pm and most others had gone to sleep already.

That night, I found it hard to get to sleep with so many details running through my mind. Did I forget anything? Who do I have to call?

What about our contact for the next town? Did I put his number in my phone? Would I oversleep? Would I even fall asleep? Relax. Rest. Take it all in and breathe deeply. Infinite hours of planning were coming together. All would be fine. Marion and I left the door to the deck slightly cracked so that the ocean breeze and sounds of the crashing surf could lull us to sleep. It didn't take long.

Before I knew it I was awake. It was dark and about

five minutes prior to my alarm going off. GET UP. TODAY IS
THE DAY. I could hardly believe it. The time had come!

6

Week One: Mojave Madness

Malibu, California to Grand Canyon National Park

*"Obstacles are things a person sees when
he takes his eyes off his goal."* (E. Joseph Cossman)

At last the time has come for our journey to begin.
I awoke just before my alarm went off around 5:00 am, an
hour after Clay's phone sounded its all-too-loud rendition of
2001 Space Odyssey and woke up half of the house. Very soon
came the buzz of excitement that filled the ocean air. We were
all busy waking up, packing, loading, eating, filling water
bottles, cleaning bike chains, and so forth as the time neared
for us to ride three miles to our official starting point. The
moment was jovial, to say the least, and smiles were prevalent.

It was just after 6:30 am, and we rolled away from
the house leaving most of our cares inside. Dad would be able
to go only a few miles with us before his flight home
summoned him back to Los Angeles International mid-
morning. It was our time to focus on the task at hand and to
meet up with Sarah from Hope For The Warriors, her sister,
Christina, and Scott, our new photographer friend. I was
unaware at the time, but Teresa, a friend of mine from high
school that lives in the area was waiting for us at the beach,
with her young daughter.

After a short three miles, we reached the Topanga
County Beach, removed our cycling shoes and socks then
walked our bikes carefully over just-washed rocks from the
Pacific's morning tide. Just as we lined up side by side in the

morning's crisp light to take some photos, a wave gently broke over an inch or two of our back tires.

Tradition states that one riding a trans-America ride must dip their back tire in one ocean at the start of the journey and dip the front tire in the opposite ocean to solidify the journey. The tide was low and the sea was calm. Brightness from the sun peaking over the mountains to our east greeted us with a brilliant smile. After several minutes of snapping photographs of this exclusive moment, it was time to dry and de-sand our toes to begin our multiple-mile uphill climb through the canyon that separated the magnificent ocean from northwestern Los Angeles. Butterflies were gathering in some stomachs as wetness stung the eyes of Ruth and Marion. The moment was surreal indeed.

After two years of planning, we were about to launch this mission. None of us knew what the road ahead had in store. With keen awareness, we knew that we would be changed in some way by this journey, but no one ventured to guess how.

Day One / June 4, Wednesday
Malibu, CA to Victorville, CA
113 miles 6,545' climbing 7:23 time in saddle 15.3 mph avg.
Hook Community Center – lodging for the night

Once we rolled over Topanga Canyon out of Malibu, we managed to thread two mountain ranges on our way to meet the Mojave Desert. We had to climb 6,545 feet on the first day as we covered 113 miles, taking us to the dry wasteland. The day was long and hard but traffic through the San Fernando Valley was light. Temperatures climbed to the low nineties before lunch and higher once the mountains were behind us. Spirits were high, despite feeling the fatigue of a big day starting to take over. Finally, around 4 pm, we made it to our destination.

Victorville sits just on the western edge of the great Mojave Desert and it is where we landed for the night. Our first night of this marvelous and life-changing adventure was spent in the Hook Community Center multi-purpose room, where a belly-dancing class had just finished. The facility was terrific; we had the locker rooms all to ourselves and plenty of privacy. Once we got our bedding setup, Clay decided to go on a ride while the rest of us showered and found a place for dinner. Seven weary riders had a Mexican meal as the sun sank into the sky to end our first day of the journey.

We returned to the community center to learn that Clay was still out riding his bike as darkness came. Moments later he called to update us: He was lost. Keith climbed into the SUV and tried to follow Clay's directions to no avail. About thirty minutes after our return from dinner, Clay had found his way back as the stars came out, one by one. Keith soon returned and we all bedded down for the night.

Sleeping in a big room all together was an experience. Reminiscent of a teenage lock-in at church, some stayed up a little longer on their devices while others were fast asleep the moment their heads hit the pillows. Some made strange noises of unknown origin and others snored softly. Some tossed and turned while others didn't (or couldn't?) move a muscle. The room was warm, which enabled sleep to come faster.

With low temperatures in the fifties, we decided not to roll out in the cover of darkness but to leave at daybreak. The daytime highs in the upper nineties were forecast to hit mid-afternoon, so we felt we had plenty of time to reach our next destination. Ludlow, California, was ninety miles away and a truck stop, hotel and Dairy Queen awaited us.

Pam and John, as promised, joined us in Victorville and planned to stay with us for a few days before heading back to Florida. She knew what desert riding was like and was prepared to help out in any way. What a great friend she was.

John drove ahead to the next destination and Pam would either navigate or drive the SAG for a few days.

Day Two / June 5, Thursday
Victorville, CA to Ludlow, CA
90.4 miles 1,490' climbing 4:43 saddle time 19.1 mph avg.
Budget hotel for the night

Breakfast on Day 2 was whatever we had in our bags: bagels, power bars and a banana. Nothing was open early enough for us so we put some grub in the tub and took off. Thankfully I had packed a small coffee maker, which proved to be very helpful along the way at times when we had no other source of the dark brown, life-saving liquid. I felt much excitement and was well-rested, ready to go. Today would be a much easier day, or so I thought.

During the first few miles we saw a cyclist coming towards us and I shouted: "Come with us! We are going to Florida!" He turned around and joined in our pace line for a little bit. His name was Dale from Victorville and we had a good few minutes of conversation. I realized that he wasn't quite on our riding level when, gasping for breath, he asked me: "Just how fast are you going to ride?" Once we hit a few hills, he was gone. Farewell Dale – and keep up the good work.

We turned onto the famous Route 66 and took a few photos and stopped for water and electrolyte refills. After riding for a few hours, we turned into the infamous Bagdad Café. I had done some research and it is a fun, touristy dump for sure. But we just had to stop for a snack. Anyone who has been on the old Historic Route 66 in this part of the desert has seen this place. It was featured in a 1987 German comedy film in which two women who were recently separated from their spouses became friends. Europeans who visit southern California often stop to visit the cafe, we later learned.

No sooner had we unclipped and parked our bikes than two tour buses of French citizens overtook the entire place. Ed hurried inside and got a table for us as the air began to buzz with indecipherable grunts and sounds from the visitors.

We should have known there was a problem when a café worker said to Ed: "You all came to EAT?" Apparently no one eats there; they just come in, take photos and buy souvenirs. The somewhat toothless hostess became the cashier and apparently didn't see the eight spandex-clad American guests sitting at the table for twenty minutes. Finally, water was brought to the table and was quickly consumed. Another ten minutes passed and the tourists abandoned the building, so I had high hopes that we would soon get to order, eat and skedaddle. Most of us decided on light fare: sandwiches, a milkshake, fruit and cottage cheese, etc. You know, something quick and easy. Right? Not at all.

While we waited another twenty minutes or so, we began to talk with a local who apparently was friends with the waitress/cashier/hostess/now-cook. We asked him "Just what it is that people out here do?" His reply, "Meth."

Fast forward to our exit: It took almost two hours for this snack stop and the sun only rose higher with the temperatures. Some team members were obviously very frustrated by this but others thought "What a cool adventure." It's all in the attitude.

We iced up, watered up and rolled out around 11a.m. with just a couple of more hours of riding ahead of us. Or such was the plan.

Route 66 has its share of stories, I'm sure. Parts of it were actually pretty nice with the big blue and white logo painted in the middle of smoother pavement. But as we headed deeper into the desert, we saw the road all but disintegrate underneath our wheels. Disintegrate may be an understatement. Loose gravel, fissures three-inches wide, potholes, uneven pavement where it crumbled over the years of baking made for a very rough -- and dangerous -- surface. I truly feared that my bike was going to shatter because the road was rougher than anything my beloved Goldilox, my gleaming, ultra-stiff, carbon-fiber Stradalli racing bike had ever been introduced to. She is used to fast, smooth road surfaces. My jaw was chattering so ferociously that I had to ride with my mouth open to avoid chipped teeth.

We could hear the slapping of our chains on the frames of our machines; not a good sound for cyclists. Two riders made better time than the other five of us so we split up a little bit. (Truth be told I think they were in a hurry to get to Dairy Queen.)

At one point our group of five could see Interstate 40 to our left a few hundred yards. We could see smooth surface with a very wide breakdown lane and it was calling our names. The only problem was that a four layer high barbed wire fence that interrupted our path to it. I said to Scott: "If we see a break in the fence we need to get to the Interstate." He scoffed and replied: "Fat chance that will happen." Within a quarter mile there WAS a break in the fence. Without a second thought, we hoisted our bikes onto our shoulders, crossed the lava field of black rock, sand and cactus and hoofed it onto the beautiful, glass-like surface of brand new asphalt on the interstate. Oh, this was heavenly. Our behinds, shoulders, hands and jaws could now relax as we rolled with ease.

We knew that Route 66 would join up with I-40 soon and we could even see our other two team members just ahead. Thankfully, common sense prevailed with them as well, and we all met up within a few short, smooth miles where there was an interstate ramp.

Finally, we could make good time again and enjoy riding. Pam and Clay stopped every few miles to douse us with water and offer some air for our tires. We found out very quickly that we traded a rough road surface for multiple flat tires. The short, sharp wires of blown steel-belted radials that littered the shoulder of I-40 became our new foe, but it still seemed less lethal than the ditches and dangers of old Route 66.

What should have been two hours of riding time turned into four, thanks to multiple flats. Our weary group exited the interstate at an intersection with a DQ, Chevron gas station and a ten-room, cut-rate hotel that was actually cleaner than expected. There was a diner next to the hotel and we had planned to dine there (after DQ, of course). We found that it was already closed for the day, well before dinnertime. I guess in the middle of the Mojave you can set your own hours.

Something that was discovered during our many stops to fix our flats was that the tires on the trailer were worn down to the core. We surmised they wore prematurely due to the weight of a partial pallet of water donated by Niagara Bottling Company in Florida. We reloaded some of it to Pam's minivan. Then Clay and Ed spent the rest of the afternoon driving back to the last town to have two new tires mounted. In the meantime, the rest of us showered and trekked to Dairy Queen to have the best Blizzards known to man. We savored every bite then went back to the hotel to wash our kits in the bathroom sinks and hung them to dry in the 100-plus degree temperatures. I swear I think they dried in 15 minutes flat. Dairy Queen was the only option for dinner so we headed back a couple of hours later and then together reviewed the next day's route, mileage, weather, etc. We also had to decide whether we wanted to try Route 66 again or make an illegal ride on I-40.

Day Three / June 6, Friday
Ludlow to Needles, CA
92.5 miles 3,074' climbing 5:45 time in saddle 16.7 mph avg.
Best Western, Colorado River

Seeking advice from the few locals that worked in the Chevron Station in Ludlow, we inquired as to the condition of Route 66 going eastward. They assured us that it did not get any better at all -- only worse. However, it is illegal to ride bikes on the California interstate and we did not want to be cited for that. We were torn. The very wide shoulder of I-40 from the day before let us rest in the comfort of knowing that we were safely out of the way of traffic while in the breakdown lane. We had plenty of room, at least six feet, where we could easily ride in a double paceline out of the way of the right lane of fast-moving traffic. Couple that with our bone-jarring and near-crashing experiences from the treacherous Route 66, and the decision was clearly being narrowed down.

We voted to take the interstate the next morning. Sometimes one must weigh the letter of the law against common sense. Route 66 was not only a horrific surface but was not safe for riding up or down the undulating hills of this desolate terrain. So at daybreak, we rode up the entrance ramp onto I-40 with the blinding sun in our eyes, blocking out any sign that might possibly have reminded us that we were about to do something illegal. We felt like we had chosen the lesser of two evils and there were no other options for riding. Hopefully we would not have to explain that to any authority who might not agree with our logic.

We started encountering flats right and left -- around thirteen total, I believe (I lost count). Have you ever changed a flat tire on a bike? Some are relatively easy to change and can take about five minutes. Other times, as is our case here, we had to search the tire for the tiny wires, as thin as hair. If we left the wire in the tire, you see, as soon as we put in a new tube, it would be pricked and go flat again. Add the frustration of one after another -- sometimes only minutes apart. When the flat is on the back tire it is more challenging to change because of the chain and gearing. Keith and Bill did many tire changes because they were quite speedy tire changers and wanted to get back on the road as quickly as possible. Both broke nails and got blisters from these multiple changes. We lost about two hours that day due to flats.

The heat only intensified on the black asphalt, and patience grew thin at times. With forty miles to go, the Garmin computer on Ruth's bike registered more than 100 degrees. We had to dodge pieces of exploded tires, burned patches of road where cars overheated and caught fire and other bits of debris; but the new asphalt was a delight and the forsaken scenery had a science fiction feel to it. Somewhere prior to a planned rest stop on the interstate as we approached Needles, I heard someone behind me say, "Uh oh, police."

My stomach sank as I recited all of the reasons why we had opted for the interstate, the main one being that the only "alternate route" was not at all usable by bicycle. I've never erred by telling the truth so I prepared myself for having to get us out of this mess honestly or cough up a stiff penalty for our decision. As I slowly peered over my left shoulder (trying to be inconspicuous for some reason) I saw the lights, the car and heard the following message from a loudspeaker: "It is unlawful to ride a bicycle on an interstate when there is an alternative route." My brain screamed out "BUT THERE IS NO REAL ALTERNATIVE ROUTE, SIR." Thankfully, my body did its own thing: smile and wave, as I often do. We all waved and nodded as he turned off the lights and slowly rolled past us. Whew. Was he going to be waiting for us at the next exit though?

Not too far up the road were a couple of state troopers, engaged in conversation, parked in the median, driver windows together, cars facing in opposite directions. I ducked down into my drops. And, when others noticed the officials, we just knew we had been spotted and were going to get it. I said, "Don't wave, just look forward and keep riding. Pretend we are invisible and they won't see us." Within a few minutes we were past them and there was no issue.

Could it be because we were all dressed in red, white and blue trimmed with stars and stripes? Could they tell that we were not just cyclists out on a group ride for fun but out on a mission? Or were they just caught up in a good joke? What on Earth did they think when they saw us? Did they even see us? It seems to me that they had to do their duty and warn us or turn a blind eye. Whatever the reason, we were grateful and stuck to our belief that Route 66 was not an option. I believe we had Divine protection that day from motorists, who were driving upwards of 70 miles per hour no more than ten feet from us for hours.

We had some challenging climbs that day; not so steep but long grades that were wearing us down. We had about 3,000 feet to ascend and the temperatures soared above 100 degrees again. At one point Ruth and I broke into British accent and role played as an interviewer and interviewee. Perhaps it was being overly tired or due to the fact that we were breathless from the long climb that we had encountered.

The entire group was laughing hysterically as we cut up for at least ten minutes. Finally I got the idea to put this on my video camera and it became a big hit once it went on Facebook. What to attribute the giddiness to remains unclear but it is a memory I will cherish for a long time. It lightened the stress level associated with flats, heat and climbing, and provide much-needed comic relief.

Finally we had completed our last big climb. We could see our destination miles below us as a green strip of oasis in the distance. Going down the multiple-mile descent into Needles, California was fun but felt as if we were riding directly into the backwash of a jet with afterburners on. The hot, dry wind was enough to make my eyes dry instantly when I turned my head to glance over my shoulder for others. Strong crosswinds toyed with us and made us descend much more cautiously than we would have enjoyed. Suddenly at one point, my bike and I were pushed two feet into the lane as a big gust of wind overpowered me. Ruth said later that she let out a scream when she thought it was going to knock her down. Her Garmin computer registered 122 degrees when we finally reached our hotel in Needles.

In front of the hotel the recognizable Route 66 logo was painted on the driveway. For fun, I laid on the iconic emblem as Pam snapped a picture. When the palms of my hands and tops of my feet touched the blazing hot pavement, I quickly pulled them off the surface with a very loud cry. I looked like a cross between a sky diver with his knees bent and arms lifted up and a fish in a frying pan. I got up as quickly as I could with tight legs from having a good 295 miles on them in three days. I got up as quickly as I could. Pam took the picture at the perfect moment, catching the image digitally. I don't think I will forget that scorching moment.

While the rooms were being readied, Marion, Ed and I peeled our jerseys off and dove into the clear pool. The water was so cold that I could only stand it for about ten minutes, in spite of being overheated from the ride. Shivers and goosebumps forced my exit from the water.

What a day it had been. We were thankful to have the intimidating Mojave Desert behind us. Despite being hot, spirits were high, team members were playful and we were going to have to gear up for the next day. Tomorrow's ride has a big ten-mile climb that will put us at a 2,500-foot higher elevation. That means the temperatures will be a little cooler on the other side of the pass. Arizona, here we come. We will welcome cooler temperatures.

Day Four / June 7, Saturday
Needles, CA to Kingman, AZ
68.1 miles   4,712 climbing 6:45 saddle time 14.2 mph avg.
Days Inn (mostly paid for by the local VFW)

After all the excitement of near-misses with our
friendly law enforcement officers, flat tires and high
temperatures, we were looking forward to a less dramatic day.
It started off with the temperature in the upper sixties, which
was quite nice. We rode due north into Arizona and crossed
the Colorado River. We passed huge fields of lavender and
alfalfa, saw mountains in the distance, and were all in good
moods -- especially after we found the Arizona portion of
historic Route 66 was quite well-maintained. We had asked the
locals at the hotel and their good feedback led us to believe it
was once again safe for riding. In Arizona it is legal to ride on
the shoulder of the interstate but when we looked at the
topography, we could save a couple thousand feet of climbing
if we went on Route 66.
　　　We encountered very long flat sections and some of
us played games trying to guess how far it was to a certain
landmark. None of us were right. During one such guessing
game the bend in the road was seven plus miles ahead. We had
guessed four. After the one big, long climb we all regrouped at
a convenience store and stuck together for many of the
remaining miles. The route was just beautiful taking us
through Bullhead City and up a ten-mile climb. Just before the
climb we made a stop at a fire station and made some new
friends, iced up, and used the facilities before we tackled that
big ascent up Union Pass.
　　　I found a great way to beat the heat was filling a sock
with ice, draping it around my neck, and then securing it with
a giant safety pin. This trick came in handy for the first week

in particular. As the ice melted it would drip down the front and back underneath my jersey cooling my torso from all directions. With temperatures in the upper nineties the dry heat would all-too-quickly evaporate the moisture. I capitalized on every opportunity to refill the soccer sock that I borrowed from our son's drawer. (Sorry Jay, I didn't think you would ever wear it again.) While the stolen soccer sock was a great way to cool off my core, I could feel a burning sensation in another body part that was a bit more difficult to soothe. A saddle sore already? But this is only Day 4. Twenty-seven more days of chaffing; this may be a problem. Despite applying generous amounts of Butt Butt'r throughout the day, my body was not used to this kind of abuse.

Three of our guys wanted to pick up extra tubes in Kingman since we made a huge dent in our supply box with our dozen-plus flats during the last two days. Each rider packed their own supply of tubes, but with so many flats we were loaning them to others. We decided to just have a bag of new tubes in the SAG and split the cost. So Bill, Scott and Keith split off as we came into town and went to a bike shop. Marion and Ed stopped for lunch and Ruth and I went on to the hotel to check in. Clay and Pam were close behind. Everyone made the big climb and all of us were pretty tired. The temperatures were much lower than in Needles, but were still in the nineties.

Chaplain Wayne of the local VFW Post was very kind and asked the Post to help our crew. They paid for three of our five rooms that night, so I called to thank him and let the chaplain know that we had made it. We had hoped to be able to thank him in person but he lives in the next town over and was unable to make it to dinner with us.

Pam's assistance, encouragement and empathy were immeasurable. At times she would drive the SAG so that Clay could get in some miles with us. That didn't alter her commitment to get water to us. She would pull over ahead of us, splash us as we went by or hold chilled bottles of water for us to snatch from her hands. Having ridden across America, she understood how we felt, what we were thinking and what we needed most. But it was that night in Kingman when she told me that she was going to have to head back to Florida earlier than expected. Tomorrow would be her last day with us. The plan changed so that she and BillyD would tag-team in Williams. Then Pam would go with her husband to make the long drive back to Florida.

We were all sad to see her leave; she was such a fantastic help to us. There was some confusion as to the reason for the change in plans but I did not feel comfortable pressing her for answers. She had already done so much for us. Her departure came earlier than we had discussed; we were expecting her help for a few more days to get us to Bayfield, Colorado but it was a hiccup we were forced to deal with. Such is often the case with something as complex as our mission. I drifted off to sleep that night wondering what other surprises might meet us on the road ahead.

Day Five / June 8, Sunday
Kingman, AZ to Williams, AZ
127 miles 5,994' climbing 7:45 saddle time 16.3 mph avg.
St. John's Episcopal – Lutheran Church

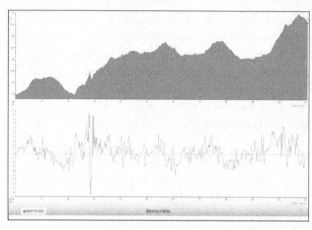

Day 5 Ele

At our team meeting that evening in Kingman, this
elevation chart from the RideWithGPS mapping program was
our focus. To a non-cyclist, this picture may not mean very
much. However, to a cyclist it is borderline frightening. The
solid block represents the elevation of hills and the numbers
up the left side of the chart reveal the feet above sea level for
every ten miles of road. We started out just below 3,500 feet
and topped out at almost 7,000 feet before settling into
Williams at 6,780 feet. The etch-a-sketch-like lines on the
bottom half of the chart tells us the actual percentage of grade
for the route. Most of the grade is 3 percent to 5 percent but it
peaks close to 10 percent. At this grade, effort to get up the hill
makes us breathe harder and our legs start to cry out in
discomfort. While climbing at this grade, we must not only
push down on the pedals but pull up as well, fully engaging
every available leg muscle, particularly at more than 5 percent.
Once we get to 10 percent, our hearts are beating quite
strongly and we are drenched in sweat.

Some were daunted by the seemingly cruel route
before us. Understandably so. We were starting to get into a
rhythm and a schedule that were good for us. Team member

Bill (not to be confused with my husband, BillyD) presented the chart above and we discussed how to tackle it. We knew that we would be faced with temperatures in the nineties. This proved to be a bit of a tense meeting where some voiced concerns of how to keep everyone together with this huge amount of ascent. It was decided that we would split up into groups of two or more, based on how comfortable we felt as we worked our way up the ten mile stretch into Williams, Arizona.

My idealistic notion that we would all "ride as one" was going out the window because, unless every team member subscribed to such a line of thinking, it would be useless to expect us all to stick together. Some team members had their own ideas of how to do this Ride Across USA and we didn't all jive all of the time. One would think that this should have been sorted out ahead of time but it was not.

The original understanding was that if someone could not stay on pace they would have to get in the SAG. But that never had to be implemented because no one fell off alone; someone always stayed with a rider who was at a slower pace and we were all OK with that. With a SAG vehicle on site it was workable since our driver could go ahead and wait for the last riders or leapfrog the team, which is what we did much of the time. Clay or Pam would even shadow us at times, when roads were particularly barren or busy. For the most part, the team was not spread out over more than a few miles on any given road.

The day proved to be a killer. We all were feeling fine for the first half of the day and had a nice lunch together in Seligman, Arizona before tackling a monstrous climb into Williams. Locals had warned us about it but hearing about it and seeing it were two different things. We met up for a short rest stop before the arduous ten-mile ascent. Moods were good, people were happy and I was just ready to get it behind me. After all, BillyD would be there for me at the restaurant in

Williams. That was my motivation to get there quickly -- without overdoing it.

Once the climb began, however, we splintered up like a piece of wood on a sun-dried deck. Bill and Scott were off the front and I worked hard to stay with them for a while, before deciding to go at my own pace. That proved to be a smart move. Ruth and Keith did their own thing. Marion and Ed had the pace they enjoyed so all was good. I found myself alone again on Interstate 40 (the only option) and having a good time suffering alone in silence. I could see Bill and Scott ahead on some of the turns, and it did not bother me in the least to have some alone time; I actually rather enjoyed it. This was indeed a tough climb that went onward and upward for a solid hour. Seeing signs for the Grand Canyon National Park eased the discomfort, and excitement flowed from my heart down to the pedals. Since I allowed distractions to take my mind off the climb, suddenly I was at the assigned meeting place and just behind Bill and Scott.

I dismounted Goldilox and every muscle in my body was shaking. I felt weak but ecstatic to know that I would see my beloved one in just a few more minutes. Within a half hour, the team reunited and rode into Williams to meet some kind VFW Post members who wanted to treat us to dinner. We met at the Pizza Factory where BillyD and three war veterans awaited us. This is also where we bade Pam farewell and told her know how thankful we were for her help. We would miss her.

After a satisfying meal, it was obvious that the team was exhausted, so we went on to the public pool for showers. We then made our way a few blocks to St. John's Episcopal-Lutheran Church, which graciously hosted us for the night. We were beat, but kept in mind that the next day's ride was a short one...and one that would take us to the south rim of the Grand Canyon.

How wonderful it was to have my husband beside me

at night. So many stories to tell but I was just too tired. There was energy only to write the daily blog, go to dinner and snuggle up to sleep on an air mattress with the cool Arizona desert air blowing through the open windows of the church above us.

Day Six / June 9, Monday
Williams, AZ to Grand Canyon National Park, South Rim
59.9 miles 2,146' climbing 4:02 saddle time 14.9 mph avg.
El Tovar Hotel for 2 nights

The next morning one of our newfound veteran friends offered to cook us sausage and pancakes for breakfast in his church kitchen. Stephen is a giant of a man whose big heart mirrors his stature. He met us at the pizza dinner the night before and suggested coming over early to feed us, and we were glad to oblige. It was terrific. The smell of thick, sizzling link sausage permeated the church hall as coffee percolated in a huge pot. Aroma of thick pancakes on the griddle danced down the hallway to where the team slept. This meal was just what we needed to get to the Canyon. Stephen is a giver and a great breakfast maker. We filled up, packed up and headed out for one of the seven natural wonders of the world. Each morning before we left we gathered around the SAG and team members read an inspirational story that had been provided by Hope For The Warriors. These stories were testimonials from those who had been helped by Hope. On this day, Ruth volunteered to read. We were again motivated by and reminded of the great cause behind our journey. We headed north and expected to have a nice, short ride with just a slight rise of elevation. It would be an easy day of riding so Clay joined us for the entire ride and BillyD drove the SAG wagon.

We rode an easy pace, taking in the scenery. With an early start, the air was charged with new-found energy among teammates. We stopped at Bedrock, Arizona to snap photos around the Fred Flintstone Campground. We saw bigger-than-life statues of the cartoon characters and a model of Fred's house. We even jumped in his car. In just over four hours our short 60-mile ride ended at El Tovar Lodge in the Grand Canyon Village. It is the only lodge in the park with air conditioning and was worth the extra expense. Our days were toasty warm now and this was our home for two nights and our first rest day. We checked in, settled in around 2 pm and began to explore the surroundings.

My husband and I walked to the rim of the amazing canyon to see it for the first time -- together. Our anniversary had just passed at the end of May so we tried to act like our time at the Grand Canyon was our celebration. It was hard to pull that off with the little ongoing project but we made the best of it with seven other friends around.

How delightful it was to know we had the rest of the day off. We enjoyed dining together, storytelling, and dessert-sharing. Then we headed to see the magnificent sunset on the canyon walls. As if we had not had enough of each other, we stayed together in the tavern where I had another silly video interview with Ruth (now known as the character of Mary Onefeather). We picked back up where we had left off three days prior, sporting British accents and talking about the "punch" that she needed in her spot of tea at the end of the day. It was puerile indeed, causing some of us to laugh until we cried. Before it got too late, our weary bodies notified us that it was time to rest. Getting a real mattress and some down time was just what we needed.

Day Seven / June 10, Tuesday – Rest Day
Grand Canyon National Park

On our first rest day some team members slept in and others met for breakfast. A few of us even braved chilly predawn temperatures to watch the sunrise over the canyon. It was simply glorious. Witnessing the colors change as the huge ball of reflection rose was awe-inspiring. This is the reward I had envisioned as I planned our route to make its way to this particular park. Despite the sweat, flat tires, frustrating moments and aching body parts we had arrived and were ready to take it all in. God's handiwork was evident in all directions, as far as I could see. The very rocks seemed to wake up in the moment as all of nature rejoiced and sang, welcoming the new day. My spirit was alive and it was a moment in time that I will never forget. Ruth, Scott, Clay and Bill sat in quiet reverence. No one dared break the beauty of the silence.

L-R: Ed Bennett, Keith Sherrick, Ruth D'Auito, Tracy Draper, Bill Bellew, Marion Kusters, Clay Smith, Scott Manning. On the morning of day 8, feeling fresh after our first rest day. About to head to Tuba City, in the middle of Navajo Nation. (Photo: Bill Draper)

The team had an entire day to spend as we wanted. Since it was our tenth wedding anniversary, BillyD and I took a helicopter tour of the canyon. Flying over the rim and seeing only sheer rock walls with emerald waters snaking a mile below was an incredible adventure. It was delightful to spend time with him and relax without worrying about responsibilities, at least for a few hours. I pray that I never take him or our relationship for granted, regardless of my dreams. It can be all too easy to do, when we get preoccupied with our own agendas.

There was a 6 pm team meeting that I had to be back for and we made it just in time. There were just a few more hours before we were back on task for another week before the next Rest Day. As a team, we gathered for another sunset. Temperatures chilled and we were thankful for the warm hoodies donated by Hope For The Warriors. Little did we know that we would need them in the middle of the night.

By the end of a long rest day, our bodies and souls were ready to trudge on. We had our breakfast time set, trailer-loading time established, and we all split into our little groups for bedtime. In the middle of the night we were rudely awakened by the incessant screams of a fire alarm. REALLY? Since these things can happen, BillyD and I were neither amused nor alarmed. We waited until a knock came on our door. We looked into the hallway and staff was going door to door evacuating guests. Noticing a whiff of something burning in the air, we did the unthinkable: We grabbed a few important items, threw on appropriate clothes (remember, it was cold at sunset?) and I heaved Goldilox on one shoulder, laptop on the other and went down three flights of stairs to the outdoors where safety awaited us.

We must have been a sight clamoring downstairs with essential items for the remainder of our trip. We could not help but laugh at ourselves, particularly as we noticed others who laughed at us. We met Scott and Bill outside. They had their share of amusement and comments to interject as well. Those jokes kept us from freezing, I am certain. A half hour or so later the "all clear" was given and we loaded up to return to our rooms. What a relief to know that the problem was under control. We could still smell the odor of the something burned but were assured that all was safe. It took a little while to settle down for sleep but we had more memories to take home with us.

Week one was behind us. The effects of riding almost 600 miles in six days was a bit of a paradox: a boost to our confidence and a drain on our bodies. The rest day came just in time. Being able to see the plans come to fruition was a delight. Seeing us work as a team was a bonus. I realized that this is what it feels like to truly Live It.

Week One Totals
550.9 miles
23,961' climbing
36H 20M saddle time
Net elevation gain: 7,056' from ocean to South Rim
16.08 mph avg.

7

Week Two: Rising
Grand Canyon National Park to Monument, Colorado

"You will face your greatest opposition when you are closest to your biggest miracle." (Shannon L. Alder)

Day Eight / June 11, Wednesday
Grand Canyon National Park to Tuba City, AZ
84.1 miles 3,209' climbing 4:29 saddle time 18.7mph avg.
Quality Inn

In just the first week, we had become accustomed to the fact that curious onlookers stopped to ask who we were and what we were doing. When we gathered for group photos or stopped for a break, we almost always had a few people inquire as the nature of our trip. This was the case again as we packed up the trailer, posed for photos on the canyon wall and readied ourselves for the day's ride. It was always rewarding to share our mission with others and they were often moved enough to donate to Hope For The Warriors. That morning we also had a nice breakfast together then rolled out of the park on a bike trail while Clay and BillyD took the main road. One problem: Ed suggested we ride the bike trail since it had some more amazing views of the canyon, but Clay didn't get the memo. It was a good two hours before we met up again and we were clueless about anxiety that Clay and BillyD faced.

The group of seven riders were having a blast

sightseeing and taking "one last picture" with the canyon in the distance. I knew that there was only one road (excluding the bike trail) to take us to Tuba City so I wasn't too worried that we didn't see our SAG for quite some time because I knew we would eventually have to meet up. Cell phones did not work in that area of the park, which further added to their stress. The rest of us were having a grand time. A couple in a convertible alerted us to the fact that our help was looking for us. Oops. Finally, after two hours of riding, we met up with the SAG as we exited the park. We got an earful from them as they shared their concerns about being out of contact with us for so long. I responded that we were not a bit concerned, as we knew there was only one road to the desolate Tuba City and we would all be on it eventually. We agreed that the SAG had to be notified if the route changed, which made sense. We chalked it up to miscommunication.

From there the riders stuck together for a while and made a plan to visit a certain hole-in-the-wall cafe for lunch. It happened to be the only gas station/cafe between the Park and Tuba City. So we thought we should stop there and rest, refill and relax a few minutes. That plan was fine until two team members rolled off the front and took on the highway construction zone without us. The other five team members had to figure out what to do so we kept moving forward, foregoing our lunch stop and met up with the SAG at a spot where there was a place to pull over. We ended up dining at the rest stop, making the best of the snacks and sports nutrition products that were packed inside. One at a time we left the SAG, except one rider who appeared to be in no hurry and even waved to me as I rolled by. With construction cones on the road, we felt it safer to slow roll and spread out within sight of each other and with enough room for traffic to pass when the opportunity presented itself. Before too long the last team member was nowhere to be found. As I caught up with two others I asked if they knew whether the straggler was OK.

I was told that he wanted to be left alone. Sure – no problem. I could do that; we all have our days; perhaps it was a DD for this one.

About an hour passed. I could see him behind me I slowed down to check on him. He flew by me as if I were standing still and he was cursing up a storm. I said to myself, "See if I ever wait on you ever again." As it turned out he was having a serious blood-sugar issue and wanted time alone so that is where he stayed. The rest of us rode into Tuba City with winds of 30 mph blowing us sideways. We convened at a McDonald's for ice cream, lunch and whatever else we wanted. The missing rider was nowhere to be found but he had texted another team member to report that he was OK. He would meet us later. I learned from BillyD that night, in the midst of a construction zone, an RV had run him off the road and into the grass, but that he stayed upright. He then wished the driver well, or something like that.

The landscape in Tuba City looked like the surface of Mars: red boulders, red sand, desolate, dry, eerie and unfriendly. The wind was just as unforgiving. The dry air cracked our nasal passages then caked them with dirt. Dust devils spun all around us. It was kind of fun to see them but after seeing five or six, the cool factor wore off. We just wanted to get out of the wind, to eat, drink and shower off. We were more tired than after a normal eighty-mile ride because of the conditions.

Tuba City ended up being the only place in the entire trip where our pre-planned lodging did not work out. When we arrived at 12:30 pm, I called the contact who had arranged for us to stay in their community center. She informed me in a cool tone that we could not come to the center until 5:30 pm. This was the first time that I had been told we had a specific arrival time. During the multiple phone calls and confirmations ahead of time, I had told the contact that we would get to town between noon and 2 pm. I then asked where we could go for showers and some relaxation until we were allowed to go to the center. She gave me the name of a school. It was just two miles away so we mounted up and headed over. One problem: wrong school. This was the middle school and we needed the high school. Thanks for the clarification.

Around the block we go -- with winds that whipped sand into our eyes and mouths and that almost blew us off our bikes. At the high school, they were happy to see us but that was not the school we needed to find. THAT school was another block or so away. It was a private one that housed groups like ours. We pressed on with fuses getting shorter by the minute. At the next school, we were greeted unenthusiastically and told that showers were four dollars and there was only ONE shower head. The team looked as if they wanted to strangle me. BillyD and I scrambled to find another option. Everyone was tired, cranky and filthy – including me.

After a few calls made away from the group, we asked the team if they wanted to stay in a hotel. The stickler was this: The only hotel options were a suite for five and two queen rooms. With little discussion, the team opted for a hotel stay. Several hours after arriving into town sweaty, stinky and cantankerous, we checked into a hotel and got some rest. What a way to come off a rest day. Emotions were elevated at our team meeting before dinner and we all needed a break from each other.

BillyD and I went to a nearby restaurant and dined quietly. The others ate together in the same place, but in the back. We did not know they were there until later, and I feared I had made a mistake by not joining them. There were so many things going through my mind that I felt I had to sort through it all. I wondered how the five roommates in the suite were going to make it work out. I wondered about my ability to lead. I wondered what BillyD was thinking and how Pam and John were doing on their drive home. No time to worry about that; we are all adults. I now had two full-fledged saddle sores to contend with that needed my attention. It felt like a third was beginning to present itself.

Day Nine / June 12, Thursday
Tuba City, AZ to Dennehotso, AZ
97.4 miles 2,828' climbing 5:29 saddle time 17.8 mph avg.
Dennehotso Chapter House

A good night's sleep does wonders for the emotional state of mind. Some of the five who roomed together had less than a bonding, slumber party experience but all emerged at dawn to get back on track. We had a mission and a plan and it was time to get about it. No time for ill wills, bad attitudes or complaints. We had to press on, no matter who was mad at whom. In twenty two more days we are expected to be at our final destination.

We were in the middle of the Navajo Nation, a beautiful desert wasteland that our Native Americans love dearly. We all know that poverty has taken over the Nation and have heard how sad it is there. The odd thing was this: The people we saw with dark skin, black hair and beautiful ebony eyes were happy and so very proud of their community. We saw poor but happy families. It was not what I expected, the happy-go-lucky faces that we encountered. Based on travels that I have taken to third world countries in the past, I should not have been surprised. The poverty-stricken Hondurans that I spent two weeks with in the 1990s had the same glee in their eyes. Perhaps the freedom of not having to live up to expectations is so liberating that these impoverished souls can live in joy, despite their circumstances. I could learn a lesson about first-world problems, which pale compared to those of third-world countries, and how they can steal our peace.

The Dennehotso Chapter of the Navajo Nation invited us to stay with them in their chapter (community) house. This turned out to be one of the best memories of the entire ride. Our hosts for the night were so beautiful:

Carmelia, Frank, his wife, Art, the children, the stunning surroundings, and their dreams for the future. There was so much more to this short stay than we saw on the surface of their dusty town, as we would begin to see that same evening. There were a few others that we met that were not the most popular in town; they were the derelicts that you read about on Indian reservations. Yet they were so kind, so interested in what we were doing ... but so lost.

Some of the buildings on the reservation were newly built with crisp air conditioning, new carpet and flooring in the office building that also housed the post office. We were shown our home for the night, adjacent to the nice, new offices. The doors to this community building were propped open with bricks and a few black flies had taken up residence within. We had access to two showers and a kitchen that was being remodeled, as well as a wifi connection.

Frank Yazzie, the chapter president, arranged for us to take a sunset drive to a special place deep in the desert. We were fed a scrumptious Native American, home-cooked dinner of fried bread, different kinds of beans, grated cheese and a special salsa-like concoction to sprinkle on top. It was as colorful as delicious and had a special southwest flavor that my palate was not accustomed to. The sun was getting lower in the sky and we were encouraged to hastily pile into a fifteen-passenger van to see "something that most white men do not get to see." We were whisked away even deeper into the middle of nowhere. Roads quickly faded into the vast terrain of hills, rocks, sand and dunes. We passed vast rock formations that glistened in the sun with a mosaic patterns of light. Rays from the lowering ball of hydrogen pierced what appeared to be shards of glass by the millions that lay on top of giant pieces of flat sedimentary rock. I inquired as to what we were seeing and was told by our guide that it was from a shameful part of the Navajo past: Broken glass from bottles of alcohol that have been there for an unknown number of years.

Our driver, Art, was taking directions from a 250-pound, thirteen-year-old linebacker who knows the area well since he rides his four-wheeler out there. The navigator doesn't speak much but instead uses gestures to point Art into the proper direction. The team is astounded and frightened as we take on eight percent grades, massive sand dunes and other desert-type landscape into the middle of nowhere in a passenger van with a broken fuel gauge. I must confess that when Art stopped the van and jumped out at the same time as our mysterious autopilot, I looked at BillyD with slight concern.

The two guides just needed to look at the lay of the land in a different perspective. So as soon as they figured out the next "road," they were back in the van and moving forward. Silly small talk amongst the team went something like this: "Oh my, what have we gotten ourselves into?" and "I hope we can make it back before dark." And "Are we going to die out here? Who would ever find us?" It was as if we had made a bad decision to come out to the middle of nowhere at dusk.

About an hour into our drive, it ended abruptly. Suddenly, Art parked the van with a lurch and we were shown a high cliff about a half mile away. What we came to see could be found once we hiked about 1,000 feet up. Trusting souls that we are, we agreed to follow our guides. Art said he was going to show us something that very few people get to see. But of course -- humans did not frequent this part of the country middle of nowhere. The sun was sinking deeper into the western sky.

We had no idea what was in store for us. A thirty-minute, 1000-foot climb over cactus, sand, ravines, rocks and unidentified scat led up to the top of a cliff and what we saw was simply breathtaking. Monument Valley lay before us to the west with the sun reclining behind it. Silhouettes of picturesque landscapes that I had only seen in John Wayne

movies came to life before my eyes. My brother had told me
about the Valley, and now it rested in its glory before me --
perhaps fifteen miles east of the Valley itself -- but
magnificent all the same. Well worth the drive and uncertainty,
I felt a little badly for not having complete trust in our tour
guides. My mind turned to the joy and happiness they had
attained by being enriched by nature rather than valuing
artificial satisfactions. We spent a good half hour on the Comb
Ridge Monocline, taking in the geological formation and
shooting photos. It was hard to make out the small white
rectangle of the van's presence from this height and distance
so we had to, again, trust our guides to get us back. Clay and
the linebacker stayed back, rather than climbing the face of
Comb Ridge. So once we found them, we knew we would be
able to find our mode of transportation back to civilization.

At the picturesque setting of the sun setting over
Monument Valley, we listened to Art share his dream for his
people. I saw in his eyes a longing for a better, more
prosperous life for his family. He stretched out his arm and
pointed northward where he dreams of having a casino one
day. He shared how he is building a dam on the reservation to
hold the monsoon rains of summer to water crops that they
will plant and harvest. With a backhoe he is digging irrigation
ditches and enlisting help of other Native Americans in his
community to improve their quality of life. How inspiring he
was and what a wonderful way to close our long, hot day in
the middle of Navajo Nation. He and Frank understand how to
Live It.

Something else that I found interesting was the
lanyard that Frank's wife wore around her neck. She is a
schoolteacher on the reservation and came over to meet us
after work that day. It's not unusual for lanyards to hold
credentials for teachers and students but this one was blazoned
with the Washington Redskins logo. BillyD asked her about
the controversy surrounding the team name and she scoffed at

it. If she, a true Native American is not offended by the name Redskins, why should others be? The day before in Tuba City, we met another Native American gentleman who sported a Florida State Seminole lanyard around his neck. Our new-found friends were very proud of their heritage and not in the least insulted that sports teams choose to use them as mascots. In fact, they both said they were proud of it.

As we met people along the way, we were fortunate enough to hear about some of their own dreams. The dreams were as diverse as the surrounding landscape and as different as the individuals we encountered. Even though we had just a short time to visit with our new friends along the way, there are many I have kept in touch with since our ride. Frank Yazzie told us of his dream, and while he did not use the term Live It, I knew that was precisely what he meant. This is a paraphrase of his history and his dream for the future of his people, according to my memory:

Frank was raised on the Navajo Nation reservation. As he grew into young adulthood, he joined the military and served more than twenty years before returning home to his roots. Currently he is the Dennehotso Chapter President of the Navajo Nation and is fulfilling his dream of going back to where he was raised to better his people, to give them hope for the future and to help them break out of some of the social ills that have kept them from reaching their potential. He is highly respected in his community and sure to continue along the path towards prosperity for his people. Perhaps that is why we saw joy in the eyes of the Navajo people that we visited.

Surely he is doing something near and dear to his heart, something he is passionate about and all the while, benefiting others along the way. That is the true spirit of Live It.

Day Ten / June 13, Friday
Dennehotso, AZ to Mesa Verde, CO*
114.7 miles 5,195' climbing 6:25 saddle time 18.2 mph avg.
* three team members rode an additional 15 miles with 2,000'
more climbing for fun that is not included in these totals Mesa
Verde Lodge

Thankfully, our accommodating hosts finagled a way to get
the air conditioner working while we were out on our sunset
field trip. We slept in the main room together, woke up before
sunrise, and packed our belongings. We walked our bikes the
half mile dusty trek in loose, red sand to a point where we
could mount up and roll northeastward towards Four Corners
and beautiful Colorado. Once again breakfast was what we
had in our supply box: crackers, bagels, nutrition bars, maybe
a banana. According to the route map, there would be a
convenience store an hour or so up the road so we were
prepared to indulge later on. Our SAG drivers went ahead to
fill the ice chest and get the water cooling. It was going to be
another hot day in the wasteland of the northeastern Arizona
desert.

The team was energetic and happy. About an hour
after starting our ride, we found our SAG at the assigned spot.
A few hours later, we stopped at Four Corners and then arrived
in Colorado. Four Corners was fun because it is where
Arizona, Utah, New Mexico and Colorado meet. The actual
GPS location is a few feet from the monument but that was no
matter to us. Several of us took pictures as we stood in all four
states at once. Some pulled a "Twister" move and put each
hand and foot in a state; I added a twist with a backbend,
touching all four states simultaneously.

Photo by Bill Draper

As we left, I turned to see one of the children copying my backbend. No doubt her back did not feel the same strains as mine.

Within minutes of leaving the monument, the landscape began to change as we crossed the line -- literally. Red sand was replaced with light colored sand, the San Juan River appeared and the climbing began again. The large, wooden state line sign that welcomed us into Colorado was smack dab in the middle of a beautiful descent. We laughed at having to stop for a team photo because the alternative was to curse it. "What doesn't kill you almost does" is a motto around our house that I applied in this situation. We lost all momentum from the downhill but joked about it instead of being upset. After taking the photo, we began climbing within a few hundred yards. The hill had a gentle, 3.5 percent grade but it never seemed to let up. From miles 54-103, we faced a constant climb. There were a few spots where it leveled off and provided us some rest. But for the most part it was up, up and away. The closer we got to Cortez, the harder the wind blew. At one point we made a left turn onto Highway 491 and got hit with a huge gusting crosswind that literally almost blew me off Goldilox. When we stopped shortly thereafter, Marion picked up her bike and held it up by the top tube so that we could see how the wind blew it sideways. Just a few miles away was Cortez, where we would stop to rest and rejuvenate before making the higher climb to Mesa Verde.

We were able to find a Wendy's where the owner of a local radio station met us and asked us to do a public service announcement about texting and driving. The studio was just a few miles up the road and on the way to Mesa Verde so we planned for me to stop there while Bill, Keith and Scott made a quick store stop. The other three wanted to get a head start on the big climb of the day. Clay dropped BillyD off with me then went back to Wal-Mart so they could put their items in the SAG. Marion, Ruth and Ed were well on their way when I met back up with the others at the radio station. The interview went well, we took some pictures at the radio station then we were back on the way.

I rode with Keith, Scott and Bill up the long, scenic road to the national park that housed famous Indian cliff dwellings. The entire group met at the entrance of Mesa Verde National Park about an hour later and we devised a plan to get us all to the hotel. Since it was at the top of the mesa about fifteen miles and 2,000 vertical feet away from the front gate, we made a plan for Clay to drive four of us up and come back for the other four. Because I had made the reservations and had the method of payment, it made sense that I would check us in. Bill, Scott, Keith and BillyD would wait at the park entrance and be in the second shuttle. The only problem was that our three strong guys did not really want to wait so they took matters into their own hands and decided to ride their bikes to the top. As if 100-plus miles weren't enough for them that day. In hindsight, I wish I had given the credit card to my husband and sent him ahead with the first group and then ridden up with the others.

Since the SAG trailer was full of other bikes, I left Goldilox behind with BillyD, Keith, Bill and Scott for the second load. Little did I know that my headstrong husband decided that the bike would be his vehicle to get to the lodge.

Now here is something that you need to understand: BillyD is an athlete but not a cyclist. But he is a very strong-minded man. When the other three team members decided to ride up he thought, "Why not?" I did not know until later that he was unaware of the mileage and climbing involved. They set out for the hotel and Keith tried to coach him a bit, warning him not to overdo it or else it would be very hard to get his heart rate back down. Within two miles, the three had left him behind, thinking that he would just stop and wait for Clay's return. What they did not know was his level of determination and that he was feeling abandoned up there on the side of a very steep and winding road that seemingly led to nowhere.

In the meantime it took us forty-five minutes to drive to the hotel, another twenty minutes to check in and another fifteen to unpack our things so that Clay could retrieve the others. Cell service was nonexistent with my provider in this remote area but Ruth somehow got a text from BillyD that he was riding up alone. We shook our heads in disbelief and knew that Clay would find him not far from the park entrance. He wore blue jean shorts, a T-shirt, Redskins baseball cap and tennis shoes. Unlike our cycling shoes that attach to the pedals on the bike, tennis shoes are no help on a bike. Cycling shoes aid the pedaling process by allowing the leg to not only push down but to pull it back up, giving much more efficiency to every single pedal stroke. My husband was clearly disadvantaged. He wouldn't make it on my tiny bike very far, especially since he didn't have cycling shoes. I believed that he soon would be with us, since Clay had gone to retrieve him. I made coffee and readied the room so he could shower and relax before dinner.

Unbeknownst to us, he had made it ten of the fifteen miles. He had done most of the hard work, climbed the steepest grades, gone through a long dark tunnel with no light and we were all astounded at his perseverance. We all went out to congratulate him on his accomplishment but he was less than exuberant. The poor man was beaten up, exhausted and felt like we all deserted him. Now that this experience is behind us, he tells the story with much greater detail and much comic relief but he was not laughing at the time.

Day Eleven / June 14, Saturday
Mesa Verde, CO to Bayfield, CO
70.8 miles* 4,570' climbing 4:25 saddle time 16 mph avg.
First Baptist Church of Bayfield
*including Mesa Verde descent for four of us

On this beautiful Saturday morning it was chilly at the top of the 8,200-feet high mesa and four of us decided to ride the fifteen miles down where we would meet the others who rode in the SAG to the exact point where they left off the day prior. Descending is such a thrill for me that I wasn't about to miss this opportunity. Going down the side of a mountain at high speeds, taking on the curves as a race car driver does, I experience a whole new rush. Not only having the wind whip across my face and arms, but tears streaming down my cheeks because of the cool temperatures ushers me into a new level of existence. I feel so alive and full of adrenalin. I absolutely love descending.

As I went down Mesa Verde's steep grades, I was again amazed at what my husband had done the day before. How did he do it? By sheer determination. The descent was thrilling but since there was some traffic and I wanted to live long enough to complete the mission, I decided to ride the brakes for most of the steepest portions. Managing to keep the speed under forty mph, I felt like that was fast enough and safe enough to keep it fun. Going through the long, pitch black tunnel offered its own brand of fun that could also be described as kind of scary.The rest of the day we saw 14,000-foot mountains with snowy caps standing tall, framing our views, much like a professional photographer does when taking the perfect picture. As I rode I took it all in -- the beauty, the experience, the magnificence of the creation. As I did almost every day to this point, my heart would race and tears would fill my eyes as I said (sometimes aloud): "I CANNOT BELIEVE WE ARE DOING THIS."

With no formal breakfast at the hotel, we rode into Mancos, where signs pointed us to a bakery. This little town in the middle of nowhere showcased old, red brick buildings that sported awnings, flowering plants and even had a rushing river meandering its way through town. While dining inside, a woman approached our table and invited us over to the VFW meeting that was about to occur. We made a short visit there on our way out of town, telling of our mission, snapping a picture or two and taking in a few more donations. We had now collected more than $8,300 for Hope. Before long, it was time to head back up Highway 186 and climb some more. We stopped in Durango for a bike shop visit and a nice lunch. We had lunch outdoors at a little cafe, drawing more attention to our group, unintentionally. The green umbrellas shaded us from the sun at 6,512 feet above sea level. Our plates were filled with colorful, healthy foods. Everywhere we looked there were potted plants boasting bright purple petunias, pink impatiens, bright orange calibrachoa cascading towards the ground. We posed for pictures, gave out some business cards with our donation website on them and answered more questions. What a beautiful place Durango is! I did not want to leave.

After a filling lunch, we made our way to Bayfield to meet our hostess and church home for the night. Debbie Renfro was kind enough to let us shower in her home and the First Baptist Church housed us in their youth room for the night. We drove over in small groups to shower in her home three at a time. How good it felt to be in a real house again. There were times when I missed the familiarity of being home with the family and our dogs.

Debbie had built the two-story home herself and, rightly so, was very proud of it. She was a fantastic hostess, even offering to let us use her laundry room. There was something special about this little town that gave it a little Mayberry feel. Could it be the hospitality? The perfectly manicured lawns? Or was it the colorful, hanging flower baskets that seemingly hung on every porch we saw? Whatever it was, it was refreshing.

Even in Mayberry, though, things don't always go perfectly. Dinner was a bit of a fiasco, as we went to a pub/ restaurant and waited over an hour for our food. So tired during the wait, I fell asleep leaning on BillyD at the outside dinner table. While we had been waiting such a long time, the sun - as well as the temperatures - had gone down. The chill in the air woke me up and when I saw there was still no food, I went inside and asked for the manager. The man I found turned out to be the owner, who made a few excuses then said our orders would be out shortly. With frustration I went back outside to our table and barely sat down before the waitress approached our table, visibly upset. With panic in her eyes she blurted out, "It's all my fault. I forgot to turn the order in. Drinks are on the house tonight." That was little consolation as our stomachs were screaming aloud for food and water was free. On to yet another Mexican restaurant by foot we went as we grumbled down the dark street. They were wonderful and had food out to us within fifteen minutes.

During the initial restaurant wait time prior to my nap, three team members found a laundromat. Hand washing clothes in a bathroom sink had become the norm so this was a treat. At least the extra-long wait time had allowed some of us to do laundry. We left the Mexican joint satisfied, with clean clothes and visions of the trip's biggest climb the next day. Some had indicated that they wanted ice cream, but the parlor was closed by the time we walked past. It was probably best to just get back to the church and get some shut eye.

Day Twelve / June 15, Sunday
Bayfield, CO to Del Norte, CO
100 miles 6, 627' climbing 6:12 saddle time 16.1 mph avg.
The Windsor Hotel, compliments of High Valley Community
Center

This day started off as our coldest one so far with
quite a nip of winter in the air for our Floridian bones. The
temperature at roll time was thirty eight degrees and we had
our highest climb to conquer: Wolf Creek Pass, elevation
10,837 feet. Prior to the big ascent was fifty five miles of
beautiful scenery taking us to what some team members feared
-- and all respected. Personally I felt very confident taking on
this challenge because I had had some experience in the
Rockies, due to a successful jaunt up a portion of Pikes Peak
in September 2013 to the 12,000 foot elevation point. Not all
of our group had ridden in the mountains before now, but our
track record for this trip had been good and I wasn't too
concerned about anyone not making it up. It was just a matter
of how long some would have to wait at the top for the others.

Temperatures climbed more quickly than we did as
the sun peeked over the San Juan mountain range in south
central Colorado. Within an hour we were shedding our long
sleeves, jackets and ear warmers. Exchanging full fingered
gloves for half ones, we were beginning to encounter some
uphill gradients. The group began to splinter, as was our norm.
Each of us found someone else we were comfortable pacing
with. Typically Scott, Bill and I climbed well together; Keith
and Ruth had their system going strong, and Marion and Ed
worked on the same level, enjoying each other's pace and
company.

Climbing must be done at one's own comfortable
pace, particularly in a long, hard ride like ours. With the SAG
close by we had nothing to worry about. It also reduced stress

among our group not to feel like some had to "keep up" or others had to "slow down."

As we closed in on Pagosa Springs to refuel before pedaling our way up the big mountain pass, we paid a very short visit to downtown where we could see the famous hot sulfur springs. If only we had hours -- not mere minutes -- we would have gladly soaked our weary legs in them to help us prepare for the tortuous climb that lie ahead. Perhaps it is better that we did not have the time; we may have never left the therapeutic waters. The very name of the tiny town, I came to learn, is from the Ute tribe that called it "pah gosah," which means "healing waters."

An acquaintance of mine came to ride with us for part of the day. Jeff Johnson lives near Del Norte, where our route took us that day In 2013, Jeff and his father rode more than 400 miles across the panhandle of Florida to raise money for Hope For The Warriors. As providence would have it, he and I met in the Villages, Florida, where his father gave a presentation to the same bike club that I had been invited to speak just seven months before our trip. We stayed in touch specifically so he could join us on this day. Jeff rolled up behind us a few miles before Pagosa Springs and it was quite fun to see him ride a fat tire mountain bike and keep on pace with us "roadies," with our skinny-tire bikes. He is strong. He was our guide on the Pass since he knew it well.

We stopped for lunch at a quaint burger stop in Pagosa Springs. Conversations at the lunch table revealed that everyone felt good; no one voiced any concerns. Once our crew was fed and hydrated, we headed East to face our test. BillyD and Clay were to check on us about a mile up the mountain, then go to Mile Four until we all passed them. Then they would drive up to the top to regroup and have photos at Mile Eight. Surely we wouldn't need any more rest stops. Jeff had explained over lunch that the hairpin turns and sharpest inclines were in the beginning.

The maximum grade is 8.5 percent and the average grade is slight at 3.3 percent since it is a major highway. The tricky part is that it never lets up; you climb, turn a corner praying for a flat piece of ground so that you can give your legs a rest but it never comes. For eight solid miles it goes up, up, and up some more. Oh -- and to top it off -- it begins at the elevation of 7,612 feet and increases to about 11,000 feet at the summit. With less and less oxygen to fuel the body as we climbed, it got more challenging every quarter mile. The lack of oxygen could cause shortness of breath, dizziness and fatigue. This could affect each of us in a different way and it was important that everyone on the team rode at their pace, being careful not to overdo it. It took an hour for the first three to reach the top without taking a single stop.

The key to successful climbing has three components: 1) attitude 2) gearing 3) strength to weight ratio. If any one of these is missing you can bet that it will be a negative experience for you, no matter how big or small the climb. It takes time, patience and practice to be able to take on mountains without feeling like you are going to die.

Over lunch Bill and Scott placed a little bet for fun: Scott, aptly nicknamed Zippy, would allow us a ten-minute head start. As the group spread out soon after lunch, the head start was in place and Bill and I were soon on our way up. We passed Ruth and Keith at the first hairpin; Ed and Marion got a big head start after lunch and were all smiles as we passed them on hairpin number two. Zippy was nowhere in sight and we think he took a nature break somewhere to ensure that we got our promised head start.

Knowing better than to redline, we had a nice easy pace of 7.4 mph for most of the trip up to the sky. As is a habit while I ride, I chatted and asked Bill lots of questions. This is how I keep from overdoing it: If I can't talk, I am anaerobic and working too hard.

In an anaerobic state, one is working too hard to

maintain the pace for very long. The human body is so amazing that it switches to overdrive and utilizes an entire different energy source. In the anaerobic state, the heart rate rises higher than eighty percent of maximal function. While it will not lead to fatal consequences for a trained athlete, one does not know how many times in a workout they can hit this level. The best thing is to ride smart and conserve energy.

After hearing how Bill and his wife met and a few other stories that I pulled out of him, I could sense that he just wanted peace and quiet. So I pulled out my handheld camera and began filming our ascent. Before we knew it we had passed the SAG twice and we were only about two miles from the top. Where was Zippy? We were about 9,500 feet up with nothing to stop us. We felt great. As we panted and took in the lovely vistas, I turned to look for the little mountain goat, Scott. About 1.5 miles from the top I looked over my shoulder to find a figure gaining on us -- incredible.

The air got increasingly thin and I decided I should save my breath for breathing, not talking. While still not going anaerobic, I could feel fatigue setting in. Slow the pace to 7.2 mph. Good move. Not much more to go now. Finding myself a little bored, I decided to take out the camera and give a little lesson on "How to Climb Wolf Creek Pass" as I am nearly breathless (mostly for posterity but also for fun). Perhaps oxygen deprivation had set in to the point of giddiness.

Before I knew it Zippy was smiling alongside us briefly as he passed by. I tried to go on with him at his pace but his 8.4 mph was not something I really wanted to maintain for a mile or so. Truth be told, I don't think I could have anyway so I settled into a nice 7.6 mph pace so I could finish the beastly pass that lie just ahead. What a wonderful sight it was to see warning signs of a 7 percent grade descent just ahead. We did it. We finished seconds apart and celebrated with high fives, photos with the Continental Divide sign as our backdrop and smiles all the way around. There was snow on the ground and the air began to get chilly as we waited for Ruth and Keith. We celebrated again with them and just a few minutes later came the last two in our group. The SAG had come up in the meantime and I dug out my jacket and full fingered gloves for the chilly descent.

Little did I know at that moment that there was some pretty serious drama between our SAG helpers and a rider, based on where the SAG had stopped. He was again having blood sugar issues and wanted the support vehicle to be there for him earlier than it was. Unfortunately, the incident affected the team for the rest of the ride. We all handled it in different ways. Most stayed quiet and kept their feelings to themselves. Others voiced their annoyance clearly. The dominant feeling was to let it go and press on. These kind of fissures happen when emotions are high, bodies are tired and different personality types collide. Lesson learned: Get on with it or get out of it. Even the healing powers of the hot sulfur springs in Pagosa might not have been able to rectify this situation, but a soak in the springs would have at least felt wonderful. Maybe on my next visit to this beautiful town.

Day Thirteen / June 16, Monday
Del Norte, CO to Salida, CO
82.5 miles 1,821' climbing 4:12 saddle time 19.6 mph avg.
First United Methodist Church Salida

After being treated like kings and queens at the Windsor Hotel for the night, it was time to pack up and move on again. Our contact for this overnight stay was a delightful young lady named Adrienne, who arranged with the hotel's owners to give us a complimentary stay in Del Norte's premier hotel. The Windsor is a historic hotel that was completely renovated and was hands-down the nicest place we stayed on our five-week journey. Chef Regan, made a special dinner for us, and they put us in a private banquet room with a few special guests who wanted to meet us. My brother, his wife, and my nephew drove four hours to see us so it was a very fun, engaging time with them.

However, as we enjoyed the specially-prepared dinner, the conversation and energy levels died out quickly because of the toll of the day's ride and other emotional stress. I could tell that this would be a wonderful place to return to and stay for days, but that was not for us this time. We were there about fifteen hours, as was the case with most of our stopovers.

Our ride to Salida was snappy at about 7,500 feet of elevation. The air was a little thin for riding fast so we slowed it down some and headed north to our next stopover, pedaling between two beautiful ranges with snow-clad peaks. A herd of mule deer got spooked by us and ran alongside us for a good mile or so. As we entered Salida on a bike trail, a half dozen horses galloped over towards us and ran next to us for a little way inside the fence as if to welcome us to town. It was magical.

We stayed in the basement of the First United Methodist Church as it had been outfitted for groups like ours. Because it was a shorter, easier day, we were able to poke around downtown, see the river and have a nice, big lunch. It was a lovely day and I felt so at home in the mountains. Marion was thrilled because she got to watch some of the World Cup and cheer on her Netherlands team as we had lunch in an eclectic riverside restaurant.

Day Fourteen / June 17, Tuesday
Salida, CO to Woodland Park, CO
100 miles 5,735' climbing 5:34 saddle time 18 mph avg.
Country Inn
My favorite day of the entire ride

Cool, crisp mountain air greeted us as we emerged from the basement of the church, loaded the SAG and rolled downtown for breakfast. I was excited about the route as it would take us higher in the Rockies where the scenery would be fantastic. We mostly stuck together until the climbing began and then broke into our comfortable riding-pace groups. Bill and I worked well together so off we went. Scott hung back to take photos and the SAG was leapfrogging ahead of us and waiting for those behind us. Chatty, as usual, I began to ask Bill questions to help pass time. His curt response was a little hurtful at first but turned out to be a blessing. "Shhhhh...." said he. "Listen to the mountains." For the next couple of hours, that is just what I did. What a story they had to tell.

We regrouped again atop a Kaufman Ridge with Buena Vista to our west and Pike National Forest on the right. The descent was a couple of miles long with a right turn near the bottom. Bill was having such fun on the descent that he missed the turn and went on straight towards Fairplay. It was amusing because I caught it all on camera as we whistled and yelled to get his attention, to no avail. He was tucked down in aero position and we were flying along at 51.9 mph, according to my Garmin.

Bill did not see the turn and went straight. The rest of us slowed down to a speed that was safe for making the turn off. Ruth and Keith decided to roll on towards Woodland Park but Scott and I stopped and waited for Bill about twenty five minutes. My sweaty clothes did not mix very well with the 50-degree temperatures and I got chilled, so I decided to roll on as well. The SAG was going to be waiting for us at mile fifty six. Scott waited for Bill, who had called to find out where everyone was. He had gone just a few miles up the road and would be back on track in thirty minutes. The plan was for Bill and Scott to reach me before the SAG but that just did not occur. The decision for me to go on solo made this the most wonderful day on the entire ride for me. A big, genuine need for me is to have a little time every day to myself. With very little "alone time", I relished it on this day.

The terrain brought with it a gradual decline in elevation. There was a huge tailwind and, at times, I was rocketing along at 32 mph on flats with minimal effort. With no one around to hear, I began singing with delight whatever came to my head. The pop song "Best Day of My Life" (by American Authors) was forefront on my mind. I felt so alive, so fulfilled. As I passed gurgling streams, I heard them offer musical praise to the Creator. I tried to take it all in: snow-capped peaks standing tall on all sides, purple, yellow and white wildflowers bobbing their heads to their own rhythm in the wind, and the mystery of what wildlife was just yards away in the forest all had me captivated. The next song to enter my head was "How Great Thou Art." I was giddy with pleasure from the vistas surrounded me. Laughter and patriotism erupted simultaneously as I was overcome with the magnitude of what we were doing for our wounded veterans. *My dream was being fulfilled!* "America the Beautiful" became the next theme song. I wept with joy and humility as I pedaled all by myself for a while. I lost all track of time and while it may have been only 90 minutes, it seemed like much longer. It was truly a glorious experience. This was how to truly Live It.

Bill caught up with me at the SAG, but Scott was happily doing his own thing taking photos. The two of us rode on to Woodland Park with minimal talking and found Ruth and Keith along the way. We passed them by and soon found ourselves climbing up Wilkerson Pass at 9,507 feet. Pikes Peak presented herself in all of her glory as we stopped for our own photos. This was indeed one of the best days -- and rides -- of my life.

Day Fifteen / June 18, Wednesday
Woodland Park, CO to Monument, CO
55.7 miles 3,164' climbing 3:29 saddle time 15.9 mph avg.
The Sundance Mountain Lodge for 2 nights

BillyD headed to the airport for an early flight well before dawn. He packed up some of the stress of our previous days and took it with him. We would meet again either in Alabama or on Amelia Island, but for now it was time for him to get back to the office before his boss felt like they could do without him permanently. He had been with us for nearly two weeks.

As had been previously arranged with the team coach, the Front Rangers Juniors Cycling team met us at our hotel bright and early this particular morning. There were about fifteen in their group and they were thrilled to get to ride with us. Five or six were teenage racers and the rest were adults. The route for the day was one of our shortest and fell just before a rest day. However, the elevation was a bit more than we had hoped. Our team was a bit weary and I had asked the leader of the Front Rangers to take us on a tour through Garden of the Gods and over to the US Air Force Academy. We needed a sponsor to get us onto Base and team leader Herb Rodriguez was retired from the Army, so he offered. Our group of twenty-plus cyclists left the elevation of more than 8,000 feet and descended into Manitou Springs then up a huge grade into the Garden of the Gods. This hill was an unexpected challenge for our team with grades of upwards of 18 percent at one point.

Back at home, our biggest hill climb is Sugarloaf Mountain, about one quarter mile long with a short steep pitch of 15 percent for only about thirty feet. Today's nasty climbs into Garden of the Gods and surrounding Colorado Springs tortured our worn down bodies for nearly a half mile at steeper pitches than mighty Sugarloaf provides. Not quite the easy day our team had hoped for. However the scenery somewhat made up for the screaming legs. The company was quite nice too. A friend of mine who has a residence in the Orlando area, as well as one in Colorado Springs, showed up in several places to cheer us on and wave a USA flag. How special it was to me to see Cindy take time out of her day to encourage the team.

On this particular day, I made a new friend. Perhaps it is because my daughters are just about grown but I have a tender heart for teenage girls. One of the Front Ranger team members was a sixteen-year-old blonde named Charlotte. I felt drawn to her as we rode down into Manitou Springs and we talked about her plans for the future. She was a sophomore in high school and making plans to race on the collegiate level. I was impressed by her skills and openness. We, too, kept in touch after our day together. She loved my golden Stradalli bike and I loved her potential and zest for life. I asked her what kinds of things she dreamt about. Here are excerpts of Colorado cyclist Charlotte Backus's account of Live It, as I learned from her after our trip.

A dream to me is a way of living your passion and expressing who you truly are.

I had been on the bike before I was six. We had the good old training wheels as I learn to balance myself around the garage.

Years went by and I tried many different things like swimming, running, violin, singing, piano, and guitar.

In 2009 a friend had a Schwinn with the good old shifters on the down tube. She let me use it, and I am once again on the bike. I had regular tennis shoes on. It took many times and overcoming fear to even start shifting as I had to pull one hand off and shift on the down tube! It took many falls and tries to get it down but eventually I came to mastering it. ...

In 2010 I started to pick up lacrosse and joined a

team. I loved it and loved to run and throw. This team was wonderful. We were all family and I enjoyed it thoroughly. I was cycling occasionally here in there with my dad as we attended Colorado's big organized bike event known as Elephant Rock in Castle Rock, CO. I juggled both sports as I went into high school. As I was in my freshman year, I joined my very first cycling team. This was the moment I started to tell my parents I knew cycling was the sport for me and I would stick to it. But they thought it was just another phase that I was going through. As the summer of my freshman year approached, I played my last season of lacrosse.

It was the first summer day I was admitted into the hospital with a condition known as an eating disorder. My summer of racing on my bike and going on my favorite organized rides with my dad was shattered like glass. I was admitted with a low heart rate in the low 20s and was almost put into the ICU. I spent two weeks in the actual hospital and 3 months in the EDU (eating disorder Unit) I couldn't walk, cycle or even go outside for many weeks. One day, one of the employees told me that I would never go back to cycling ever again and my parents were told that may be even too hard to let me cycle again because that's what cycling was, "a way to lose weight." I was in such disbelief when I heard this. I told my parents multiple times that it wasn't that way to me. Cycling to me is a way to escape all of the first world problems and leave it all behind, in the dust, in the wind. Cycling is the way to clear the mind and learn to understand who you are as you have time with you and only you. It tests one's ability to go beyond measures.

Being told I would never cycle again made me only want it more. As I was graduating from the unit in early September 2013, I was allowed to walk a certain time every day. I would walk every day and, as the months progressed, I was back on the bike pedaling to success. I never let anything get in the way of this dream and I would never let it happen.

The length of time on the bike progressed and I was able to cycle for longer and longer. By this time my parents started to realize that I had a burning passion for cycling and it was like no other. The summer of 2014 I began to race, winning 4 state championships in road racing. I started to race with category 4 women and never set foot back at that hospital. Passion to me is what makes you, you. It's what makes you flow as yourself in this world. It makes everybody special.

I am using my passion to help others because I think having a passion allows you to expand your ability and reach out a hand to help others pursue their passion. I love helping others and it is so much fun to volunteer and help younger cyclists improve their ability and love for cycling. We relate more and have more in common to share the love for the sport and that's why I love helping others. I am using my passion to help others by being very open to younger cyclists who are just getting into the sport and lending extra information as well as some of my things. I volunteer and help at camps for junior cyclists which I am actually doing this weekend and I love doing it! I think it really feeds the sport and opens people's eyes to how cycling is more than just a sport but it is a way of freedom.

After the Garden, more hills met us and, on our way to the Academy, there were a few understandable complaints from team members because we were indeed exhausted from days of big climbs and being at altitude. Thankfully the next day was a day of rest -- we just had to survive a few more miles. A whirlwind tour of the Base and Chapel (the most visited place in all of Colorado, mind you) were on the agenda but a lunch break at Subway came first. I could tell that the team was not nearly as appreciative of our field trip as I was, but then again, they had no connection to the Academy. A few photos here and there, quick commentary on the terrazzo, cadets' dorms and other features of campus were highlighted. How I had hoped to be able to share our time in town with my son, but as military duty would have it, he was in San Antonio at the time on a training assignment.

As I stood by the chapel, overlooking his dorm, I took in the scenes around me. I missed him but felt a special gratitude for his service to our nation. I looked across the terrazzo and took in the scene of retired Air Force jets on stands, as if they were about to launch into the sky. I looked at various parts of the campus, where my youngest son was living out his dream, and taking it all in. I was having a very special Mom moment, when my eyes fell on a monument made from twisted pieces of the World Trade Center wreckage. My heart was touched and I thought of the day the world changed.

That moment was sobering.

Most of the wounded veterans that we were riding for volunteered their service to the nation after 9/11. Again my thoughts turned to them, to the cadets who were giving their lives for our freedom and my tendered heart was grateful for every single one of them. My son is among those who have volunteered to give their lives to protect our national security. What a proud moment that was for me. As I wiped away a tear or two, I came back to the reality of our team and mission. We were just a few short miles away from a cozy hotel for two nights and one rest day. Indeed, we were ready for a break.

As we rode a few miles north towards the hotel, the skies grew angry and threatening from the summertime temperatures. Some wanted to hurry up and get checked in; others seemingly wanted to enjoy the refreshing rain. About thirty minutes later, we arrived at our home away from home for two nights, where the marquis displayed a sign that read: "Welcome Ride Across USA! " That was heart-warming and much appreciated. My son's host family (through USAFA) had invited us over for dinner that night and we obliged. It was wonderful to have a delicious, home cooked meal with friends that I knew. We were tired but so happy to have a special dinner, prepared for us.

Day Sixteen / June 19, Thursday
REST DAY in Monument, CO
Sundance Mountain Lodge

For two nights and a day and a half, we stayed in a very charming hotel called the Sundance Mountain Lodge, just north of Colorado Springs. They gave us a special rate because of our cause. Over dinner that night we decided to take the cog railway up Pikes Peak (rather than trying to ride up it on bikes, like a few of us had discussed).

Ed's wife, Julz, had joined us in Salida and had a rental car. We piled into two cars after breakfast at the lodge and headed to my favorite mountain. We had a wonderful trip up the old railway and enjoyed each other's company. Even on our day off, we wanted to be together. Going through tough times can bring that feeling about.

For many reasons this enormous chunk of rock is dear to my heart. Childhood memories of an August snowball fight in the early 1970's with my family atop Pikes Peak are etched into my mind. Visiting the summit in the late 1990s with my parents and my own small children was another special time. Perhaps one of the most monumental trips to the top of that glorious peak of granite was in 2009 with BillyD. I was goofing off on a thirty-foot snow pile in the main parking lot at the top and slipped on boulders. I wanted to be the tallest person on the summit, and for a few moments, I was. On my way down the snow/sand pile both feet went out from under me and I landed with a boulder intruding into my lower back, rupturing a disc between my fourth and fifth lumbar vertebrae. The pain was equivalent to having a baby naturally, but I had a triathlon in three weeks so I didn't have time to baby it, but kept pressing on in my training plan.

Two months later with little relief, I went to a renowned orthopedic clinic where it was advised that I should stop running. At that time, I reassessed what I could do and focused on cycling as my main sport. In September 2013, I visited my favorite mountain again to bike up to the top but was forced to stop short of the summit due to three feet of fresh snow that fell overnight. It was good training for the Ride Across USA and I'm glad I could at least get to that point, given the storm that had blown in during the cover of darkness. On this rest day, I would go to the spot where I was injured and have a moment of thanks. Who knew at the time of the fall how it would change my life?

I am a firm believer that everything happens for a reason and that if you look for it, you will find good -- even in bad circumstances.

That question turned my thoughts to those we were riding for. How did their lives change after their injuries? How many of them are able to see the good come from something bad? How many other people in this world have tragedy occur that they seemingly cannot get past?

Week Two Totals
710.2 miles
35,627 climbing
39H 12M saddle time
Net elevation gain: 7,664' from ocean to South Rim
18.1 mph avg.

8

Warriors' Wish

"If you want to live a happy life, tie it to a goal, not to people or things." (Albert Einstein)

Each day during our ride, Hope For The Warriors provided us with testimonials from their Warrior's Wish program. Having spent numerous hours researching Hope as a possible beneficiary of our Ride, I became truly moved by many of their stories. It became very important to me to help our team understand the "who" behind the "what" of our mission and to inspire us during the challenges that we would face on the ride. So I requested thirty one stories, one for each of our riding days.

Anne Barnwell, who has served as the Communications Director at Hope, and I worked pretty closely together in the months leading up to our departure and she selected stories that were some of her favorites, with our journey in mind. I knew that the media and others we encountered along the way would have questions for us, so it was important that everyone have an idea of what Hope does and the lives it touches. Little did I know, how important these stories would become to me each day. In the same way that our team came with varied personalities, these stories impacted each of us differently. Some testimonials were very touching and others were less dramatic; all were transformational in the lives of their authors. Perhaps the story that spoke the loudest to me was about Zach Briséno. It resonated with me throughout our journey during difficult periods.

Here is the story of Corporal Zach Briséno, USMC (Ret.), printed with permission from Hope For The Warriors:

> *Zach Briséno is a native of Fort Worth and joined the Marine Corps in 2004, just after his high school graduation. In 2007, after serving in Okinawa and also Fallujah, Iraq, Zach returned to Fallujah as part of a police-training team. On Nov. 29, 2007, an improvised explosive device (IED) detonated under a vehicle that contained him and two other Marines. He lost both legs and injured his arm.*
>
> *While still in recovery, Zach joined Team Hope For The Warriors and completed the 2008 Marine Corps Marathon on his new hand cycle. The last leg of the race route was uphill, so the finish line could very well have been out of reach for him. Exhaustion and doubt, however, were no match for his determination. Zach made it up the hill -- not by hand cycle -- but by standing up to walk his uphill battle. The crowd was stunned by the grueling scene of what seemed impossible to someone who was severely injured less than a year prior to the race. For Zach, this was one of many examples of his tenacity and endurance.*
>
> *Since this experience Zach has exemplified the warrior spirit by pushing himself seemingly beyond human limits for these events. After he completed the marathon in 2008, Zach returned with three other Marines in 2009 to guide a double amputee, who was blind, through the Marine Corps Marathon.*
>
> *This has been an exciting time for Zach and his family. He joined the Wounded Warrior Amputee*

Softball Team and travels across the country playing the sport he loves. On March 10, 2014, he married Stacey in a ceremony surrounded by friends in Las Vegas.

Imagine: Four wounded warriors -- one of them blind -- hand cycling or running through the Marine Corps Marathon course when they might have otherwise lived out their lives in a hospital ward. Imagine how each one of them felt with arms screaming in burning pain from turning the crank for twenty six miles. How humbling for all those who witnessed Zach's finish-line experience. What images raced through the mind of the blind double amputee as he could only smell, hear and feel the energy of the race? How did it feel emotionally for them to finish?

The route of the Marine Corps Marathon is not a flat course; in fact, it has quite a few climbs. Couple that with physical issues that complicated their efforts and the result is a grueling effort by the physically-damaged vets who dare to take on the challenge. These men and women do not simply strive to finish a race like this. They come to conquer. It is programs like this that restore hope and a sense of being in the lives of those who may want to give up. Imagine how it must feel to lose a limb or have haunting voices in your head. And then imagine how incredible it must feel to overcome such obstacles with friends alongside.

The Warrior's Wish program works to inspire wounded vets and instill in them hope for the future. Applicants submit a formal application and, if accepted, funds are made available for them to pursue their dreams. Here is a sampling of the stories we read aloud on the road:

• A widow wanted to attend a weekend retreat with other women who have lost their spouses in war.
• An injured veteran who was an alcoholic living in his car

sought help and got it, under the condition that he attend Alcoholic Anonymous meetings with a Hope representative.
• A Marine captain, who had been stripped of his ability to fly after suffering a lost leg and severe burns during a failed training exercise, was able to continue his dream and get a civilian pilot's license through A Warrior's Wish.

There were so many accounts of psychological wounds from the horrors of war that plagued many who returned home. The programs provided through Hope For The Warriors deliver the opportunity for dreams to come true for our most deserving. In 2013 over 4,000 individuals and families were aided by Hope programs.

Hope has dozens -- if not hundreds -- of stories of real people with real needs that are getting met through their programs. Indeed, we chose the right organization. More Hope stories are at: http://hopeforthewarriors.blogspot.com

Check presentation to Steve Bartomioli of Hope For The Warriors (Photo Bill Draper)

Bits and pieces of these stories captivated my mind as I was having my own difficult moments on a couple of hot and windy days on the bike in Kansas. By having true stories like this to help me re-focus, I was able to get my mind off my own temporary discomfort and think about what our injured military personnel go through on their own road to reclaiming their dreams. Numerous times during our trip, these stories proved to work just as I had hoped. Our team members repeated them to curious inquirers along the way, and I am certain that they were inspiring to those people just as they were to each of us at some trying moments along our way.

Despite injuries and devastating circumstances, it was amazing to me to hear stories of how these service members and their families continue to dream and find ways to see them to fruition. At times when so many give up hope, it is refreshing to learn how a grassroots organization can provide ways for dreams to become true once again. For those who want help, and know where to go to receive it, there are many ways for them to Live It. Hope is in the business of making wishes come true for thousands of our most deserving.

9

Week Three: Rocky Mountain Highs and Lows

Monument, Colorado to Augusta, Kansas

"A dream doesn't become reality through magic; it takes sweat, determination and hard work." (Colin Powell)

Day Seventeen / June 20, Friday
Monument, CO to La Junta, CO
155.75 miles* 3,002' climbing 8:42 saddle time 17.9 mph avg.
Koshare Dance Museum (complimentary)

How amazing to try and comprehend that at the end of this day, we would be at the halfway point of our ride. Malibu seems so far away, as does the thought of arriving on the beaches of northeastern Florida. The reality did not hit me until later in the trip. There was still so much to digest leading up to this point. However, I did feel sad that we were leaving the Rockies behind. Not knowing what lie ahead, I felt a bit blasé about the upcoming days.

This was scheduled to be our longest day of riding for a few reasons: (1) some team members are Randonneurs and had to complete a 200-kilometer ride in June, (2) we would have a net loss of altitude that was more than 2,500 feet, (3) we had just come off a rest day. Again there was a little issue with the route, which we had changed from the original one to accommodate the Randonneurs. It had been altered by a team member to take us on a dirt-bike trail, as well as Interstate 25, for quite some time. This just did not sit right with me, so I began to ask local cyclists to see if there was a safer way. Two other team members and I looked at a different route and chose it to be safer, but it would add about fourteen more miles. It did indeed add more miles *and* more climbing, which was not a popular choice. I wish I had not felt so darn responsible for the safety of the team but I did. The day was a bit stressful, but I stood by the decision.

The route took us right through Colorado Springs, which was kind of fun, and out the southeastern side of that town and into the middle of nowhere before cutting south toward La Junta. We made a little mistake and missed a turn, but it added only three miles to our day. Funny how different Garmin models display the same routes differently at times. We started off with nice, cool temperatures, but we began to bake around lunchtime. There were no convenience stores and no place to escape the sun -- even for a few minutes. The landscape was barren, dry and downright ugly once we got out of the hilly terrain. Moods reflected the dull surroundings, and it was apparent that this was going to be a long, hard day. Winds picked up and blasted us from the southeast, challenging us all the more. At one point, about halfway through the route in the middle of Colorado's own hades, Bill and I were pulling our double paceline and in the distance we saw dust coming off a road ahead of us. We looked at each other and he glumly said, "Is that a dirt road?" We hoped that what we thought we saw was an illusion. We did not need to face a dirt road, particularly after we had agreed that the route change was necessary. The satellite route view did not reveal a single dirt road. For a short time I practically held my breath out of fear, but the road turned out to be paved with a little sand on top, kicked up by oncoming traffic. We both breathed a sigh of relief that the road was paved and would indeed get us to our next stop safely.

During the hot ride, my mind began to wander in order to break the monotony of the landscape and our duty at hand. I thought of how my tan lines are getting really developed despite Bullfrog sunscreen. Because of issues with dryness due to the high desert, my nasal passages had begun a revolt and some unbelievable objects ended up in the tissue no matter how many times I blew my nose. I pondered what it must look like up inside that cavity then decided that I really didn't want to know. Since my nose was perpetually clogged, I did a lot of mouth breathing. I felt something odd in the roof of my mouth and found that the uvula (you know, the little punching bag that hangs down in the back of your throat) had become plastered to the roof of my mouth. Do you know how awkward it is to try and unstick it with your tongue? I tried for several minutes, even swishing water around in my mouth before the small piece of flesh came unglued. Many other things interrupted my thinking but I shall spare you the details.

The lodging for this night was something I had looked forward to for quite some time. The Koshare Dance Museum often took in groups for the night. They had showers, a kitchenette and lots of sleeping space. It is a two-story building that houses a museum and a circular dance hall with bleacher-like seats surrounding it. Traditional Native American dances were performed on a regular basis. I was looking forward to getting to see some of the museum pieces and to learn a little more about traditional dances. As the day wore on, I accepted the fact that I would have to learn by reading online because we would be too tired to stroll through the museum by the time we arrived, much less be able to watch the show at 7 pm. How we all longed for the showers to remove the caked-on, dried and cracked dust that enveloped our bodies.

At 5:30 pm we finally rolled into the museum parking lot that was filled with cars and buses. We were sedately greeted at the door by a woman who told me that the dances were starting soon and that we could not check in until the show was over – around 9 pm or so. This did not go over well with any of us so I explained to her that no one told us we would have to wait until nine o'clock to check in. I also implored her to understand that we had been on the bikes since 7 am and that we were hot, tired and stinky. I then begged her to let us at least rinse off. After some desperate pleading, and after she got a whiff of us, she relented but told us we had to take very fast showers. So that is what we did. For now we were homeless and famished, but at least we smelled a little better.

We were told that around the block was a good Mexican restaurant. Our tired legs got us to the parking lot, only to find a "Closed" sign on the door. Groans erupted from the group knowing that the next place was a mile away. Clay opted to get the Pathfinder for those who wanted to ride instead of forcing achy legs to walk further.

The escapade continued as one restaurant after another was closed, too far away, or did not match the palates of our exhausted team. Eventually we all ended up at the same Chinese restaurant. Scott ate three bowls of rice with his entrée and the plate before me was piled high with cashew chicken and vegetables. I devoured it in no time. We then drove back to the museum satisfied and ready for bed. It was now after 9 pm, so we checked in, set up on the stage and readied our bedding for some much-needed slumber. It was then that I was told that we were also sharing space in the museum with a Boy Scout Troup. This was fitting for the type of day we had endured. Like a mama bear protecting her cubs, I boldly set out to find who was in charge of these teenage boys and make sure they knew how tired and potentially cranky we might be. It appeared that they might have had a similar day, and they assured me that they would have their lights out by 10 pm and be up and gone just after 5 am.

Thankfully they were quiet, well-behaved and kept in their own space. What else should we expect from the Boy Scouts? I felt a little badly for assuming that teenage boys might happen to act like, well -- teenage boys. All lights were out in no time and we heard not a peep from anyone. The night at the museum was one to remember -- but not because of a comedic movie, but for a comedy of errors.

Day Eighteen / June 21, Saturday
La Junta, CO to Syracuse, KS
107.4 miles 1,362' climbing 6:40 saddle time 16 mph avg.
Syracuse Christian Academy (complimentary)

With some much-needed deep sleep behind us, we were up at 5 am and going to breakfast in town before continuing eastward toward the heartland. We had learned of a neat little diner that lived up to its reputation. Wisps of steam danced skyward from our coffee cups and evaporated into the cozy atmosphere. There were smiles and happy faces on most of the team members as locals curiously eye-balled this group of eight in spandex. Words above other tables were spoken in hushed tones while we talked in full voices of what the day had in store for us. At least, what we knew of it.

Today's route was much flatter and we would be bidding farewell to Colorado. One more state behind us.

Our host for the night was Pastor Joe Gould of Syracuse Christian Church. He would be waiting to meet us later in the afternoon at the Black Bison Pub, which his son owned. But first we had to battle wind gusts of close to 30 mph and some paceline stressors. I had to fight a skirmish of my own that was taking place just underneath my helmet. This was the toughest day for me physically and mentally. There were many times that I felt so alone and this was hard. My thoughts turned inward and, for a couple of hours, I allowed them to take over. The voices in my head said all sorts of things to me and it felt like they just may be right. My left foot fell asleep every day now around the 40- to 50-mile point. Numbness in my left shoulder blade began to show itself and my lower back tightened up relentlessly. The joy of riding in the mountains that I loved so much had faded; this was becoming more like work than fun.

Not once did I think of quitting, nor did I doubt that I could get in the miles and complete the mission. But I second guessed the team that I had put together. It was obvious that there were different agendas at play, and it hurt me that this was the reality. It was confusing to me how poorly we worked together in the wind. It was as if everyone wanted to find their hiding place and were not willing help each other in the wind very much. So I dropped out of the faux paceline and rode for miles hanging off the back. At one point Scott came back to check on me. He said, "Is something wrong, Tracy?"

I replied, "No. I'm fine." His response is one that I will never forget. "Well, your face tells me something is wrong." Scott has a very kind quality about him that is very charming and disarming. With his comment I had to smile and tell him what was annoying me so. As a good friend does at times, he didn't try to make excuses or fix the problem. He just listened. And I felt somewhat better, at least emotionally. My body was feeling pretty beaten up.

There was a mishap in a small town that caught us all off guard. The main road through the tiny community of Holly, Colorado was narrow. A small truck passed with the "Wide Load" signs on it, and I turned to see what the wide load was. I was alarmed when I saw a huge piece of farming equipment rolling towards us fully taking up both lanes! When I announced that we had to really get out of the way quickly, the others also turned to see what the big deal was. Suddenly a side street presented itself as the only option but we did not notice until too late that it had a bunch of loose gravel on it that was several inches deep. I had not made it to the side road yet but was in the curb of the main road when I saw trouble.

Ruth and Scott wiggled their way uncontrollably in the gravel. Scott dipped to the right in front of Ruth and the next thing I saw made me shout something to the effect of "Oh No!" She was airborne and her front wheel was perpendicular to the curb with her back wheel in the air, as if it were a bucking bronco who threw his rider. I quickly stopped and leaned my bike on the first tree I could find and when I got back to Ruth she was lying in the curb, facing the opposite direction and visibly shaken. The others were right there with her. Marion sprang into action as our on-site nurse and gave her the once over. Within a few minutes she was upright and able to walk to a shady spot.

Furious that a city would be so negligent as to leave such gravel on the road I called 9/11 to report this. A concerned neighbor came over and told me that a motorcycle had recently crashed in the gravel, seriously hurting the driver. Do you think the police ever came? Nope.

I digress. Back to our story.

That was the turning point in my mind when I realized my thinking had to change or else the misery would continue. This small incident could have been so much worse. We were thankful that Ruth ended up with only a skinned knee, blown innertube, cracked top tube and shaky nerves for a few miles; but no broken bones or other serious injuries. She had packed a spare bike in the SAG wagon so what could have been a ride-ender for her worked out beautifully. Ruth mightily showed a character-trait that I knew she possessed -- perseverance. Lesson learned: How quickly these things happen. We all decided to work together better and look out for each other more.

Finally in mid-afternoon, we made it to the Black Bison Pub for snacks and relax time. William Royer, a

Vietnam vet and friend of the pastor's came to meet us. William is also a writer and photographer. He shared one of his writings about when he was evacuated from Hanoi. What a story written in rhymes and descriptive terms of what the evils of that war were like through his eyes. He also gave me a beautiful black and white eighteen-inch by twenty-four inch original photograph of rural Kansas Highway 50 with layers of clouds filling the sky. It is titled "The Loneliest Highway" and the rippling road that fades into the distance has on it but one vehicle as far as the eyes can see. I cherish it because it reminds me of my own turbulent day in the heartland. It was a lonely day indeed but was improving as the hours continued.

As we were leaving the pub, Pastor Joe opened up his home so that we could do laundry and shower before dinner. He had planned on feeding us buffalo burgers from his own herd back at the church. The hospitality we were shown had a beautiful simplicity to it, as did the scenery on our first day riding across a very long state.

Another day was in the books.

Day Nineteen / June 22, Sunday
Syracuse, KS to Dodge City, KS
104.52 miles 1,079' climbing 5:51 saddle time 17.8 mph avg.
Dodge City YMCA

The day started early with a paceline lesson on the dry erase board that is usually used for scripture and Sunday school lessons. Indeed, we needed some divine intervention if we were going to continue in this wind. Symbols scribbled with a black dry erase marker reminded us all of how to properly work together for everyone's benefit in a paceline. As if some had not heard this before, it was explained, gently at first, that if you wanted the benefit of being sheltered that you had to do your part and help shelter others: "If you can't do

that then ride on your own and fight the wind by yourself."
This statement was a harsh reminder of the purpose of riding
in an echelon. While no one wanted to hear it, we all needed
to. Hopefully this lesson would help the group; otherwise, we
could be at each others' throats.

Would you believe that, after just a few delightful
miles, the winds were calm? We had very low and variable
breezes that remained so all day long -- divine intervention
indeed. The skies were clear and temperatures were in the
upper sixties and low seventies. It was absolutely marvelous.
Hope was restored in my heart, and I believed we would have
a peaceful day. We stayed together most of the time and
chatted away the miles here and there.

There were many sights to see: huge grain silos,
millions of yellow wildflowers, rolling farmland, big barns,
thousands of cows in pens ready for slaughter. At one point we
warned the cows: "RUN. Run for your lives!" as they stood
shoulder to shoulder with no clue as to what the future held for
them. A part of me felt badly for the cows who were packed
into stockyards so tightly they could not even move. It was
then I realized that this is the unflattering side of
consumerism. They were livestock, property and a way of life
for many residents of Kansas.

My lower back decided that it wanted to act out again
for some reason today. It was hurting badly enough for me to
ask Marion for a patch from her medical kit to help alleviate
the pain. Again my left foot had gone numb after mile fifty
and the icy needles were again showing themselves in my
back and shoulder blade. The saddle sores that began on day
four were doing their fair share of crying for attention also. It
was a good thing that my mind was settled so that these
disruptions were considered nuisances as I tried to focus my
attention back on the story we had recently heard of one of our
Hope For The Warriors heroes. He certainly had more to deal
with than I did, so I had no reason to gripe.

When we got to Dodge City we quickly found a
Dairy Queen where we could reward our efforts. This was
becoming a pattern, and we all would begin talking about ice
cream when we had about twenty miles left in the day. As had
become my customary dessert of choice, I requested and
received a medium Blizzard with one scoop of Reese's cups
and one scoop Butterfinger bar. For the first time in my life
calorie count and fat content meant nothing to me as I
blissfully savored every single bite. I can still recall how good
each bite tasted and how the cold, creamy substance felt as it
made its way into the middle of my over-heated body.

As soon as we were all done eating it was time to
remount Goldilox. One quick touch of my fanny on the seat
reminded me that the sores were very much in need of help.
Not to be vulgar in any way, please allow me to say that it felt
like sitting on a bag of gravel with cactus thorns mixed in. It
was excruciating. I was so glad to be almost done for the day.

That night we were staying in the YMCA that was
only about three miles from DQ. Big, angry, gray and black
clouds were being stirred up by the wind and packed into
corners of the sky. Loud claps of thunder came in from the
distance and we decided to get a move on -- and fast. My
lower back and saddle issues were quite the bother, but they
took a back seat to getting out of potentially dangerous
weather.

Just as we unloaded the last suitcases from the trailer,
the bottom dropped out of the clouds and we were in the midst
of a Kansas summer storm. Huge claps of thunder shook the
air for hours on end. Soon the SAG was surrounded by water
five inches deep. Shower time was followed by growls of
hunger. We decided to order pizza and have it delivered, rather
than attempting to take the Pathfinder into bad weather. Keith
owns several Domino's stores and it is always funny for me to
watch him talk about ordering pizza. "I like to compare the
competition," he told me once. As we scarfed down boxes of

Papa Johns in the foyer of the YMCA, Bill announced that he had found a scale and that it was time for a team weigh in. Of course this occurs after I wolfed down half of a pizza. I decided to weigh anyway and found that I had lost six pounds so far. A girl's delight! I celebrated by having a refill of Dr. Pepper then went to see what Clay, Marion and Ed were up to in the kid's playroom.

Sprawled out on the brightly-colored kid-friendly carpet, Clay was snoozing as the other two watched the World Cup with delight. I got busy writing my daily blog and checking the radar to see if a tornado was coming. Indeed, there were some tornadic cells in the area, and I drifted off to sleep that night around 10 pm wondering if we would have to add a Kansas twister to our experiences.

Day Twenty / June 23, Monday
Dodge City, KS to Kingman, KS
112.6 miles 988' climbing 5:19 saddle time 21.2 mph avg.
Kingman Christian Church

We woke up to clear skies, debris on the ground and cooler temperatures. The storms had been a blessing in disguise as a summertime cool front had passed through. Later, we learned that a tornado had touched down on Pastor Joe's bison ranch, but that there was no damage, as it was in a rural part of the county.

A year prior to the start of the ride, I began reaching out to chambers of commerce in the towns that we were going to pass through. Far more often than not my request for lodging was welcomed warmly. There was one staff member at a chamber in particular that went far beyond the call of duty. She was a very kind woman named Wanda in Kingman, Kansas. She took special interest in our mission and cause.

Within two or three email exchanges I found out why: Her son had endured multiple deployments to Afghanistan and suffered from severe post-traumatic stress. While he is doing much better now, he had been through some very difficult times. Wanda and I struck up a friendship that grew over the next year. She will not take credit for what she did to welcome our team, but our brief overnight stay in Kingman was one of our favorites because of her involvement.

It began with meeting two American Legion Riders whom I had gotten in contact with via Wanda. Joe Wolfe (Polar Bear) and Shondra Kostner were waiting for us on an entrance ramp to Highway 400 East. They were very easy to spot clad with leather chaps and handsome leather jackets and the chrome on their fancy motorcycles shining brightly. Sporting sunglasses and huge smiles they were waiting for us in the breakdown lane. We pulled up behind them and exchanged salutations and handshakes underneath the warm June sun. I recall being a little emotional as they cranked their hogs' engines and started off with three-foot by five-foot American flags flowing in their wake.

There were some fifteen miles of horn honks, waves, thumbs ups and shouts of encouragement from the passengers in motor vehicles as we rode along the shoulder of Highway 400 toward our destination for the night. It was about 3 pm and any fatigue we felt from the miles behind us had vanished in a sea of adrenalin. Before too long we passed a highway construction zone that lasted for a long stretch of highway. Some workers stopped what they were to doing to offer their approval by ways of applause, whistles and shouts. Our red, white, blue, stars and stripes cycling kits garnered much attention as we rode in a loose double paceline down the highways and byways of our beautiful nation. That was certainly the case as we pedaled our way across America's heartland.

As we came to the outskirts of quaint Kingman,

Kansas, the traffic increased a bit. Out of nowhere, two police cars waiting on side roads turned on their lights, blipped their sirens, pulled out in front of our motorcycle escorts, and led the way. It was amazing! Drivers pulled their vehicles over and stopped. Some people exited their cars to see what the fuss was about. A few minutes later a large, red-brick, historic church appeared to the left. I recognized it from Google satellite. That was our host home for the night and its property was lined with five-foot flowing American flags on poles temporarily planted in the ground. A crowd of people waved flags and clapped for us. It was impossible for me to hold back the tears. Overcome by emotion I could not help but feel that we did not deserve this kind of welcome but that it belongs to those who return from service as injured warriors. It was truly a humbling experience.

We turned into the church parking lot and thanked our escorts while meeting our hosts for the night. My new friend Wanda was easy to spot: She had teary eyes and a glow about her. There was another tear-stained but smiling face that belonged to a man whose son was stationed in Germany and had previously served in Afghanistan. He was deeply touched that complete strangers would ride bicycles from coast to coast for our military. The moment was very special indeed for us.

A reception awaited us inside the church's gymnasium. Home-baked cookies by the dozen, a spread of other yummy snacks, beverages and patriotic table settings on a dozen tables showed us that many people in Kingman cared about our mission and us. Locals sat with us, thanked us and asked a multitude of questions. A writer for the Kingman newspaper was there with pen and pad in hand, patiently waiting to talk with our team. The owners of G&S Caterers came by to take our orders so that they could return later with our made-to-order dinners, complete with a vegan meal for Ruth and gluten-free for Marion. Members of Kingman Christian Church and Pastor Joshua Bell were so gracious to us and it was very much appreciated.

A World War II veteran whom I shall call "Mr. John" stopped by as well and I had a delightful thirty-minute-or-so conversation with him. He asked for a photo of the two of us so I promised I would email him later that evening. "I don't own a computer nor can I even turn one on," he said when I told him that. He had some amazing stories to tell about his piloting in WWII in the Asian theater. But he was more concerned with what our current service members are doing in today's wars. I felt honored to be able to spend time with him. This was one very special memory of the dream ride. Good for my word, I printed off a hard copy and mailed it to him after we reached the Atlantic.

We all settled into the huge gymnasium with our bedding in the various spaces that we claimed as our own, lining the walls but still close enough to each other to know we were a team. As I drifted off that night my mind danced with images of the tremendous welcome. The VIP treatment was unexpected, but very much treasured. Wanda out did herself. How blessed we were by our new-found friend from a tiny town in America's heartland.

Day Twenty One / June 24, Tuesday
Kingman, KS to Augusta, KS
70.0 miles 1,139 'climbing 4:05 saddle time 17.4 mph avg.
Lehr's Motel, 2 nights

The next morning the celebrity-like treatment continued as we met Wanda, Joe and Ronnie Fankhauser (Fang), at a charming restaurant in downtown Kingman. We were served up delicious home-cooked vittles, and hot coffee. We were asked to sign banners to welcome home local military personnel from their deployment. We shared photos with our new friends and filled up our stomachs with biscuits, gravy, eggs, pancakes and the like. As we went up to pay for our tabs we learned that someone had already taken care of it for us. Gratitude etched itself across our faces and hearts and spilled over into big hugs and smiles. Before we knew it we had to continue our journey on Hwy 400 East into the sun. With Polar Bear and Fang leading the way again we headed directly toward the rising bright ball in the sky.

It was a partly cloudy morning and our motorcycle escorts got us ten miles up the road before having to return to their planned activities for the day. The original route that I studied and planned was again changed by the team member whom I had asked to review routes for dirt roads, traffic and other safety issues. Apparently he wanted to shave off some miles by taking a direct cut through downtown Wichita rather than go south of the city, as I had planned to get us off the main highway. Instead, a few locals told us that, given the time of day we were riding on Highway 400, we should be OK if we took the highway through town. My contact in Augusta, who happened to be the mayor, warned me otherwise. She told me that it was a very fast, high-traffic, multiple-lane highway through the center of town and we needed to avoid it. After discussing the options, the group decided to take it anyway because, after all, non-cyclists seem to think that almost all roads are dangerous. We had made it more than halfway across the county and it had been fine; we would take Highway 400.

As we approached downtown, signs posted on the roadside notified us that we were now on the "Wichita Flyover." I immediately became a bit nervous. There were concrete barriers on both sides of this six lane highway and the speed limit was 55 mph. The "shoulder" was about four-feet wide and full of debris. Before we knew it, we were a part of the traffic pattern -- only we moved at a fraction of the speed of the fast-moving cars, trucks and tractor trailer rigs that moved us with their draft as they flew by. Very soon it became apparent that we had made a very poor choice. But we were stuck. We had absolutely *no* business being on that road.

Thankfully, because we were dressed alike and it was obvious that we were insane, vehicles began to give us space. Lanes merged into us from the right and soon became exit ramps. Drivers, who were no doubt in shock, gave us lots of room as we crossed these ramps and got to the next shoulder. It's a wonder that a policeman didn't flag us down and scold us. There was nowhere to go but forward as we endured several miles of the scariest ride of my life. I prayed and sang "My Life is in Your Hands" (by the Brooklyn Tabernacle Choir) for protection and begged forgiveness for being so stupid.

I rode almost all-out the entire time, completely on adrenalin. This was most definitely a "fight or flight" scenario. I felt a mix of fear and exhilaration -- sort of like being a teenager doing something naughty and getting away with it.

Out of nowhere vertical grates began to appear in the very small riding space in which we were confined. Each one threatened to devour our wheels whole if we allowed them into our path. They caught us by surprise -- so much so that one team member broke out his amazing bike handling skills and bunny hopped over the first one. The rest of us merely swerved to miss them and were successful in narrowly avoiding the danger. We didn't mind not having the pizazz that Bill showed. We were just happy to be upright. He, however, looked pro.

It seemed as if this stretch of highway would never end but, to our delight, it did. I was happy to bid this freeway farewell -- even more so than the horrendous Route 66 that beat us up in eastern California on Day Two. At least on that road I did not fear for my life.

We chose this particular exit because we needed to get to a bike shop. Our reward for the death-defying experience was to mosey around in the Bike Xchange for about two hours while some had their bikes worked on. While in the store I asked the owner for a safe way to get to Augusta, which was only about twenty miles away. He suggested a much nicer, safer and more scenic route but would add less than ten miles to our ride. Would you believe that some had the nerve to complain? Let's see... a few extra miles or another dance with death? The choice was clear to me. We took the safe route this time.

We made it to Augusta and the Mayor was there to meet us at the hotel. She arranged for the Augusta Visitor's Bureau to provide vouchers to offset the cost of our hotel expenses. How nice. We checked into a very modest, locally-owned motel that we would call home for the next two nights.

The highlight of our time in Augusta was with Mayor Williams. How special we felt that this dignitary would meet us at the hotel. She definitely fits the description of "big things come in small packages." By spending just a few minutes with her, we could tell that she is a mover and a shaker. With a very likable personality, we hit it off quickly. We all walked across the street to have lunch and meet with a reporter that she had lined up to interview us. It was during this time that she confirmed what the political yard signs were announcing "Kristey Williams for State Representative." Once the interview was done and photos with her were taken, we went back to the hotel where she announced that she would be back to pick us up at 6:30 pm for dinner at her home. We had about three hours to relax, clean up and get ready to be pampered.

As promised, Mayor Williams returned for us in her Suburban, piled a bunch of us in it and took us on a quick tour of charming downtown Augusta. A light rain was falling as we drove down the cobblestone road of old town Augusta. The slapping of the windshield wipers forced her to have to speak louder. She has played a big role in reinvigorating the town. Many new businesses were open, pretty awnings were on each store front, making main street inviting to shoppers. Soon afterward, we pulled into a beautiful neighborhood in heavier rain and into the driveway of her striking home. She had a fantastic dinner spread for us and we just about cleaned her out. Soon the city manager, police/fire chief and probable next mayor came over. As she was running for State House Representative, she called her campaign manager to come by as well. We had such a great time laughing, telling stories of our adventure and getting to know each other better. Times like this are what made the Ride so special. I felt as if I had made a friend for life.

This one-woman-show heard of our Kingman welcome by reading my blog from the day before and would not be outdone. The next morning she had police escorts to show us out of town as well. One such escort was the brother of a wounded service member whose story touched our hearts. I did not attain permission to share it, but please understand that we have many wounded service members whose injuries impact the sufferer and their families as well.

So many people we met along the way have family or friends who were involved in Iraq or Afghanistan. Hearing these stories along the way gave me renewed purpose to push on. So many needed the help of Hope For The Warriors and it became my personal mission to spread awareness of how Hope helps so many.

Since our stay in Augusta, we learned through the magic of Twitter that Mayor Kristey Williams would not be mayor for long. She took her newly elected House seat in January 2015. Remember the "probable mayor" from dinner that night? His name is Matt Childers and he won his election easily.

Day Twenty Two / June 24, Wednesday
Augusta, KS REST DAY
Lehr's Motel

Today dark skies opened up and the heavy rain gushed down. Thankfully it didn't affect our rest day plans of sleeping in. We had endured a long week and planned to get much-needed sleep, go shopping, relax, or just do nothing.

With so many kind people we had met along the way, I knew I needed to begin writing 'thank you' notes and that is how most of my day was spent. One such note was to a very generous woman from Pratt, Kansas. She met three team members as they stopped for lunch and saw the banner and signs on the SAG outside. She wanted to find out more about the mission of Ride Across USA. She listened intently and asked some questions then made a request: "May I make a donation?" Marion enthusiastically said, "Yes!" In no time, she wrote a check, turned it face down on the table, shook the hands of Marion, Clay and Ed before leaving the café. When the check was turned over the trio was astonished. It was to Hope For the Warriors for $1,000.

The day off was spent by each one taking care of their own business: doing laundry, going to the store, resting, tooling about the town between rain showers, and even doing some of "nothing." It came at a time when we needed it.

Week Three Totals
551.2 miles
7,461' climbing
30H 37M saddle time
Net elevation gain: 5,692' from ocean to Kansas
18.1 mph avg.

10

Week Four: Heat in the Heartland
Augusta, Kansas to Dyersburg, Tennessee

"Permanence, perseverance and persistence in spite of all obstacles, discouragements, and impossibilities: It is this, that in all things distinguishes the strong soul from the weak." (Thomas Carlyle)

Day Twenty Three / June 26, Thursday
Augusta to Parsons, KS
109.34 miles 2,169' climbing 6:05 saddle time 18 mph avg.

Under thick clouds and with two police escorts, we said farewell to our new friends in Augusta and continued our trek eastward on this Thursday morning. Some of our friends joked on Facebook that it is never good to be escorted out of town, but were grateful for the attention it drew to our cause. The sixty-seven degree temperature felt good and we were well-rested from our day off. We had only one more rest day until we met the Atlantic. How could it be going so quickly?

We were greeted by fresh smells as the scent of yesterday's rain still lingered. It was nice to see the landscape change before our eyes. Fields became sparse and features called "trees" began to sprout up along the roadside. Keith is the one who noticed that trees had been absent for some time. He was always looking for shade so he was overjoyed that it would now be abundant.

The terrain known as the Flint Hills brought us a few rollers, diverse fauna and more interesting scenery than we had witnessed in the past few days of riding. Kansas had been a surprisingly pretty state to ride in and offered the kindest people that we had met so far. We could understand why it is called the "heartland" with so many generous and caring citizens. Thankfully the aches and pains that wrought my body as we entered Kansas a few days before seemingly disappeared. As we rode our way eastward, it felt as if many of our concerns were left behind also.

The city of Parsons had offered us accommodations in their community center. We rolled up in front of a pretty, single-story brick building atop a small hill in the early afternoon. The enormous pool, complete with slides, was teeming with children as it sat just outside the windowed multi-purpose room that now held our belongings. The building was energized with a dozen teens and pre-teens, curious youth who peeked at us like we were some sort of new exhibit. Several inquired about our goings-on so we entertained them with some stories. Interacting with the hundreds, perhaps thousands, of people we met during this ride was a highlight of the trip for me. The entire team seemed to enjoy it. There were so many times I was very proud of the group, despite normal dynamics that can complicate this type of adventure. Each team member was chosen to be a part of the team and had something unique to offer it.

Some went to the pool as others showered and relaxed. Soon, hunger pangs took over and we asked around for dining suggestions. Hearing of a delicious Mexican restaurant just a short drive away, we piled into the SUV and headed over. Scott and I took our places in the very rear -- our own special seating place that was normally used for cargo.

There were no seats, only a small forty-five inch by thirty-one inch space. Being the smaller of the team members, it was just cozy enough and we learned to sit with our knees facing different ways so that each had just enough of our own personal space.

Dinner was yummy and lights were out at a decent hour. Rolling time of 6 am would come soon. At this point we had not tired of Mexican food; it seemed to be available no matter where we were and the salty chips became somewhat of a staple for us.

Day Twenty Four / June 27, Friday
Parsons, KS to Mount Vernon, MO
94.87 miles 3,478' climbing 5:46 saddle time 16.5 mph avg.

In earlier planning, I had tried to interface with another town nearby for a place to stay in Missouri, but it was not going very well. After repeated attempts to reach out to the local chamber had failed, I wrote one final letter in hopes of securing a place for the night. Until that point, I was told by the contact person: "I will let you know..."

That same contact person replied to my final email saying: "Our municipal buildings cannot be used for overnight activity. The church I asked cannot accommodate you. There is one hotel here so you may want to contact it. Good luck." Not quite what I expected from a chamber of commerce. Perhaps he was having a bad day. But it didn't dissuade me for long.

I began a search for a friendlier town and found that Mount Vernon, Mo. seemed to be a good fit. Their charming website all but invited us to stay there, so I reached out to the city administrator, who was very welcoming. Max Springer was a gem. He worked with the mayor, who set us up in their community building and arranged for transportation to their city's Red White & Boom celebration, which was scheduled for the night we arrived. Mr. Springer acquired meal tickets for the team and showed us where to go for the big celebration. On stage the band recognized us in front of the thousands of people who came to celebrate Independence Day one week early. It was a fun night indeed. However, before the fireworks started, we knew it was time to turn in. We had a big day the next day. It would start with a 6 am breakfast with Max.

I had hopes of getting to visit the Missouri Veterans Home, the largest in the state, where hundreds of veterans from wars of long ago reside. Time passed too quickly that day and I was disappointed not to get to shake the hands of the men and women who served for our country in World War II, Vietnam and elsewhere. If I ever get to do this ride again, I will take ten weeks to do so and enjoy more along the way.

During the ride that day, we faced 15- to 20-mph crosswinds that made the cloud-covered day a little less fun for riding. But something stood out to me when we passed a house, in the middle of Nowheresville, Mo., that flooded my mind with images of raising my young children. As we came down a nice little hill, I saw a house on the left with a red Jeep in the front yard. It was the child-sized, plastic Jeep that little people play in and pretend to be big people. It was just like the one my children had. All of a sudden, memories of Chrissy and Jay driving the vehicle around the back yard took over my mind -- and heart -- and moments of special memories took over. I could hear their laughter as they chased after Ollie, our English Springer Spaniel, in the back yard. Memories of them playing on the wooden playset that my dad put together came to mind.

I also recalled how they painted pumpkins for Halloween on the back porch and how bothered I was that Jay painted his all black (he was only three). I spent a long time reflecting on my two little ones and compared them to where they are now in life and I was both happy and sad that those days were only a memory. Happy because they are now grown young adults making their ways in the world, and sad because I miss those days when we had so much fun together.

Once we arrived in Mount Vernon, we stopped for lunch in the cutest restaurant: The Red Barn Cafe. It had the appealing country decor, complete with hens, roosters and red gingham checked table cloths. The team did a great job of replacing the many calories burned riding into Missouri. That was easy to do in this place. The desserts were double-sized and quite laden with calories, I'm sure. The homemade southern cakes, pies, brownies were big enough to split two or three ways, but a few of us managed to handle one alone. For the first time in my life I could really eat everything and anything I wanted with no guilt and still lose some weight.

Day Twenty Five / June 28, Saturday
Mount Vernon, MO to Cabool, MO
104.6 miles 4,659' climbing 6:37 saddle time 15.8 mph avg.
America's Best Value Inn & Suites

Mr. Springer treated us to a hearty breakfast with gravy, biscuits, and eggs. His hospitality made me think: "Surely we are still in Kansas." But we weren't in Kansas anymore. We were heading into the Ozarks of southern Missouri. Once again, overcast skies protected us from the hot summer sun and tamed the temperatures. The scenery is beautiful here. Five thousand feet of rollers, wild flowers galore, interesting rock displayed on highway cut-throughs, friendly motorists and windy, partly cloudy skies greeted us. Just over six and a half hours of pedal time netted us 104 miles and more memories for our trek across the USA. We dodged horse droppings in the shoulder as we spotted Amish homesteads and even an older couple on horse and buggy on the highway. There were signs posted about the town with silhouettes of such buggies, warning drivers to share the road. I was tempted to take photos of some we saw but did not out of respect for the culture; they do not like to be photographed, we had been told.

The wind was not our friend today. We hunkered down and tried to protect ourselves and each other for mile after arduous mile. My brain played games with me during the first half or so of the ride. Negative thoughts overtook my normally chippery and positive outlook. Feelings of inferiority, insecurity and frustration were creeping in to attempt to take up residence in my mind. At times I was able to combat them and change my thinking but there were long moments that I stewed on them. Finally, after the first few hours of allowing myself to "go there" (and some with some encouragement from Marion) I was able to process those feelings and remind myself that they were just feelings and not reality. This is what a lack of good sleep and punishing your body can do to you. I determined that I was really just overtired and that everything was magnified and out of proportion.

When I fell and injured my back in 2009, the MRI showed quite a bit of trauma to the spine over the years: an old compression fracture, three dehydrated discs, a ruptured disc, bone spurs, arthritis and mild stenosis. The physician warned me to not let my core get weak or I would need surgery. At the time, he said because of my fitness level, he would not dare operate, but that one day I would probably have to come see him. Cycling has done wonders to maintain my core strength, but after so many miles, day after day, the muscles that provide stability for the spine were beginning to flare. There is no doubt that my physical discomfort contributed to the battles that would plague my mind from time to time.

Along the route today, we found the birthplace of Laura Ingalls Wilder and stopped for photos before pressing on to the metropolis of Cabool. Prior to checking into our hotel, however, we managed to find a Dairy Queen and you know we had to stop. Not only was the frozen nutrition a delicious way to end our ride so often, but it was a terrific time where we could relax, laugh and just be ourselves. Somehow ice cream just hit the spot for us and never got old; or could it be that amaraderie went hand-in-hand with such deliciousness is what we didn't tire of?

A tremendous storm hit after dinner bringing crashing thunder and crackling lightning. We viewed a fantastic light show from our hotel windows. Our rain-soaked kits that were hung outside to dry before dinner had just been rewashed. We all kept a vigil and prayed that the storm would dissipate before the next morning. How fortunate we had been, riding for twenty four dry days. Had our luck run out?

Day Twenty Six / June 29, Sunday
Cabool, MO to Doniphan, MO
103.9 miles 6,056' climbing 6:29 saddle time 16 mph avg.
Rocky River Inn

As was our routine, we met for breakfast in the hotel lobby and watched the weather. There was an area of storms right in our path, but it was not wet at the hotel. Under a thick blanket of fog, we donned our reflective wear and turned on headlights. With red blinking lights on our seats, we implemented our plan for the day. Clay stayed close behind us in the SAG with his flashers on as we met hill after hill and the skies grew darker rather than lighter. Thankfully, we had a very nice shoulder to ride upon and traffic was sparse. After an hour or so, little droplets of water from the low-lying clouds turned to mature raindrops. Before long, we were in the midst of a torrential downpour. Peals of thunder rolled overhead as water splashed from our tires below and up into our faces. Road grit found its way into my mouth and lodged between the small gap in my front two teeth. Raindrops on the outside of my sunglasses made it more difficult to see than riding without them, so before long they were tucked into the back of my jersey. I then got the full spray off the wheel in front of me, but at least I could see better than before. I was able to steer clear of the rooster tail of road film and water for the most part by staying just to the left of the wheel in front of me. Dodging raindrops was a bit more difficult, but was the best option. It was our first -- and only -- wet riding day. We felt fortunate and a couple of us even enjoyed the change that rain provided. Temperatures were in the upper sixties so, as long as we were moving, it felt good. At one rest stop, though, we became so chilled that we had to warm up with convenience-store coffee.

"There is not one flat piece of land between Cabool and Doniphan," exclaimed team member Bill. But what glorious scenery adorned the roads. Twisting, turning and winding roads through fields of wildflowers near the Mark Twain National Forest made this day one of my favorites despite the 11 percent grade we faced at one point near the end of the day. This was a day of many special memories: passing a tiny country church with four cars parked in front, hearing off-key singing to an electric piano streaming from the wide open front door, racing each other up and down the hills because there was no traffic on these country roads. The rain cooled us off and a few of us got frisky like little pups after a bath. The miles finally led us to our hotel and the rain ceased. Unfortunately, so did my Garmin 510. Somehow water got inside it despite the rubber piece that is designed to keep moisture out. I spent the remaining miles of our trek with no computer to report my whereabouts, speed or heart rate. To be honest, I found that quite liberating once I got used to it. I discovered that I had been tethered to the Garmin and that, at times, it had become my identity of sorts. Sometimes my overall average seemed to dictate my confidence level. This man-made numbering system could at times control me, eating away at the sheer joy of cycling for what it was meant to be -- a pleasure. At times these devices add pressure to a ride, other times they are useful training tools. For now, however, I would get to ride unshackled from any sort of keeping track of speed or distance. And it felt wonderful.

The hills were extremely fun because of how one fed right into another. No sooner would the hill bottom out before it would head right back up, not unlike a kiddie roller coaster. None were very steep and if we hit the gearing and momentum just right, we could stand up and catch the hill in such a way that we lost almost no speed. Up and down, down and up, for hours on end. What fun it was.

Day Twenty Seven / June 30, Monday
Doniphan, MO to Dyersburg, TN
114.8 miles 1,837' climbing 6:38 saddle time 17.3 mph avg.
Holiday Inn, two nights

There was little-to-no fanfare about our cause, or our journey, after we left Augusta, Kansas. It must have been due to the fact that we hardly saw anyone but ourselves. These days of riding were quiet and restorative. I knew, as we got closer to home, things would change so I tried to take advantage of the quiet hours of riding by doing some introspective thinking.

On this particular day we would pass through three states: Missouri, Arkansas and Tennessee. We would also ride across the mighty Mississippi River, and we were looking forward to that experience. As soon as we hit the northeast corner of Arkansas, the hills flattened out and tall pine trees popped up all over the place. Arkansas was beautiful with bold green hues on the ground and bright blue, clear skies. Huge farms with soybeans, potatoes and unidentified crops surrounded us. It was obvious that this part of the country had recently seen heavy rainfall, due to acres and acres of crops that sat in brown water, so deep that the crops were swallowed alive. It was a beautiful sunny day, and we were having a good time finding turtles on the roadside and rescuing them from certain death. We must have been bored out of our gourds, but it was fun and took our minds off the endless miles ahead. If I recall correctly, Scott said we saved seven turtles.

We crossed the state line back into Missouri again and stopped for lunch at the Round House Cafe, which was the only place open. It turned out to be a nice, little hole in the wall that was very close to the banks of the muddy Mississippi. We arrived twenty minutes before closing time, which happened to be 2 pm on a Monday. The owner came over to learn more about us. She was very kind and hospitable. It didn't take her long to tell us about her son who was on the Miami Marlins professional baseball team. One of her regulars treated us to fried pies with ice cream for dessert. How did they know we loved the cold, sweet treat? This place had its own shabby charm, complete with empty paint buckets that doubled as legs underneath the booth to hold it off the ground. Silver duct tape strips covered the splits in the aged vinyl seats of several booths in the middle of the room. The owner took our photo and had us autograph a piece of paper so that she could frame it and add it to her collection of notables who passed through her restaurant. Did I mention how good the food was? We all had a fun time and commented on what an interesting stop that was. Thankfully we didn't have much farther to go.

Within six miles we were up and preparing to cross over the Mississippi River. Seeing fluorescent, spray-painted notes for cyclists on the pavement, we felt good about taking the interstate bridge, which was the only way to get to Dyersburg, Tennessee. There was no other road or ferry for many miles in both directions. One attention-getting graffiti sign caught our eyes: "USE CAUTION CYCLISTS!" It screamed at us just seconds before the danger was in view. Huge, vertical grates that could easily swallow a front wheel whole were just feet away in our path. Some riders dismounted their bikes; others maneuvered around the holes. All were safe, thanks to the warning.

It became apparent that we were in the South as Confederate flags popped up from time to time. Churches claimed their place on street corner after street corner with messages of encouragement to seek a relationship with God. Billboards proclaimed the pro-life message and "Jesus Saves" appeared on more than one occasion on roadside signs. Ah -- the South. How I love the sweet comfort and memories in my heart and mind from being reared in the Bible belt.

A short time later we were in our hotel and someone asked how we got to town. We replied, "Over the bridge." They said it was illegal to ride bicycles on the interstate. Hadn't we heard this before? Our response was that there were road markings specifically for cyclists. We were then told about recent charity riders who rode on the interstate with police escort. Oh well ... what's done is done.

Day Twenty Eight / July 1, Tuesday
REST DAY in Dyersburg, TN

Can you imagine the cumulative effects on our bodies from doing what we were doing? As good as we felt and with spirits high, we could not deny that our legs were very tired. To one, the thigh was tender to the touch. That is a sign of overtraining. To another, little aches and pains crept up earlier and earlier in the ride each day. Another had a little less patience and was a bit more anxious to get the ride done each day. One who was a huge eater became more efficient in terms of the fuel he needed to power through the day and, suddenly, he began eating like a normal human being. Bill reminded me that I looked thin and encouraged me to eat more. Marion was down at least twenty pounds. So 600 miles a week was taking a toll on our brains and our bodies.

It was our final day of rest before the end of our journey. After breakfast Bill, Scott and I visited a farmers' market and downtown Dyersburg. We ran into Marion, Clay and Ed there who rode the short four- to five-mile stretch. What a lovely, quaint town. Ruth and Keith spent their day quietly together. As usual, we decided on dinner logistics. Finding a delicious Italian restaurant, we ate our fill before going on an ice-cream search later. Between dinner and ice cream, I curled up and fell asleep in the rear of the Pathfinder.

Week Four Totals
527.4 miles
18,199' climbing
31H 35M saddle time
16.7 mph avg.

11

Reality Check

"There is no excellence uncoupled with difficulties." (Ovid)

I would be remiss to make it sound as if this dream has been *all* dreamy. How unfair it would be to all readers to lead you to believe that every day was smiles and sunshine. No -- this was a very realistic dream; one complete with thorns, bruises and a few tears. No doubt you have come to this conclusion as you work your way through the chapters. If I may, I would like to give a bit of insight to where some of the stressors may have originated.

The physical aspect of riding a hundred miles a day for thirty one days was the big unknown for each of us, since no one had ever pulled off such a feat. The youngest team member was forty three and the oldest was fifty six. We are not spring chickens. However, it became quickly apparent that the demands on my muscles were slight compared to the high-velocity strains that would arise in my mind on certain days. Each day we had hours off the bike to rest the legs; but my brain never got to unplug. Even when my body was so tired at night, I would lie on my air mattress or hotel bed while my mind raced with thoughts of: what needed to get done, where we would spend the next night, what media needed to be contacted, who said what to whom and what to do about it. A word of criticism by a teammate, or other stressors that came along the way, worked their way into my tired brain. Each night I got about five to six hours of sleep and had to cope with it the best that I could. There is no script for planning and executing a bike ride of more that 3,000 miles for a team of cyclists so they can honor the heroes of this country. While I know that I may not have always made the right decision, I did manage to make the best ones I could at the time. Some had good results and one or two became valuable lessons to keep in mind for future endeavors.

Anytime eight people get together in a cooperative effort, one can expect some challenges. Add to that the importance of the worthy mission we set out on, and the stress of the obvious physical challenges we faced. All in all, we got along quite well despite occasional unflattering attitudes, wide mood swings and infrequent spats. These things were most likely exacerbated by the compounded wear and tear on our bodies. Think about multi-day road trips sharing the backseat with your siblings and multiply that by whatever number you chose.

As we began the ride, it became evident that some on the team had their own ideas for the ride, which caused strain sometimes. I tried to put myself is each team members' shoes: They have given their resources and five to six weeks of time to achieve what would probably be their biggest accomplishment of their lives. They had skin in the game and their own expectations. That too was OK in the long run, but some stress may have been prevented if we had all discussed our expectations ahead of time. That was my fault for not doing so. Each person had his/her reasons for wanting to be on the team. I tried to focus on my own pursuits while keeping us all moving forward. I thought: "Nothing is going to keep my dream from transpiring -- no one's attitude, no distractions, and no other obstacles." The trait of a strong will was a blessing this time. With that said, there were many moments of peace and even lots of fun in the midst of the chaotic schedule.

Imagine what this might be like: Leave your job, family and friends; pack strategically for more than five weeks of travel in wide-ranging conditions; live out of a suitcase five times longer than most vacations; sleep in open rooms with acquaintances; awaken at 4 am or 5 am daily; eat food that is not your usual diet while making the best of it; put on your best face for the media and people you meet when you're exhausted; trust your leader; ride your bike for 100 or so miles daily; check into another hotel daily; keep up with your stuff; wash your cycling clothes; eat; sleep; and repeat for thirty five days. Throw in some media appearances, finding friends along the way, riding with other clubs occasionally and sticking to an arduous schedule.

Just getting decent sleep on many nights was difficult. Some snored; some tossed and turned; some stayed up late with lights shining from their devices. Sometimes, however, other noises became a comfort to me, although I can't speak for everyone. Devices for "continuous positive airway pressure" (CPAP) and intermittent compression (ICDs) rhythmically sang night after night, lulling me to sleep. The soft humming of these machines was a mechanical chorus, with their own continuous melodies that complimented each other quietly with their distinct ebb and flow. Many nights I had dreams about being at the ocean. I wonder why?

On a typical day we would get up around 5 am and ready ourselves for the day: apply chamois suit up, have coffee, eat breakfast, pack up our overnight items including air mattresses and bedding, load the trailer, review the day's route, plan rest stops, read our inspiring story and hit the road. We would ride about thirty five miles typically and stop for a bit. Refuel, refresh, fill bottles and head out for the next segment of thirty-plus miles. Repeat three times until we either found a place to have a late lunch or go on to our destination for the night. We would then check in, move in, shower up, wash out kits, relax a bit, meet for dinner, review the next route, go back to our sleeping place and relax a bit more. Occasionally, our rides were short enough for us to have a few hours to explore our surroundings. These few hours were fun, but they were not frequent. We found several towns, like Durango, Pagosa Springs and Salida, Colorado, where we wished we could have lingered longer.

On occasion we were met by a host or hostess who kindly set us up in their church, community center or school. As tired as we all were, the team was gracious to them as well. It touched me as I watched each team member consistently be so courteous to others despite fighting fatigue. How much we appreciated the hospitality shown to us by good people who took time from their busy lives and even sometimes shared a bit of whatever wealth they had. At times it did lend a little more stress to have to be "on" for our new friends. But it was not a high price to pay for what they were doing for us. Overall, we worked through the stress of constantly being with each other while creating many fond memories throughout the journey we endured together.

These experiences that we shared as a team -- both good and bad -- have shaped our journey. In time, any frustrations we had with each other will fade away as new memories take over that space in our minds. We will forever be bonded on a certain level because we got to see the good in each other -- as well as unflattering sides of others that we like to keep to ourselves. All made contributions to the team in some way and all of us saw misgivings of others. These traits balance each other out and we are all still friends of varying degrees. As in real life experiences with families and friendships, there will be some falling outs, and those who tough it out become stronger because of the trials.

Along the way, this life-altering experience benefited from a few respites. We found our most relaxing nights were in hotels with some much-needed privacy. When BillyD wasn't there, I roomed with Marion and we always had a good time. She and I became closer as we shared expectations, complaints, a few tired tears or stories of the day. BillyD was with us for almost two weeks (from Arizona to Colorado), then again at the end. It was great to have my husband at my side, particularly at night when I could hug his warm body instead of a lifeless pillow. He helped me and the rest of the team by updating Twitter, driving the SAG so Clay could ride and for being available for us overall.

As with any great feat there were some challenges along the way. Even though I was disappointed with issues that arose from time to time and how they were handled, I had to put them behind me and moved forward. We all did. Forgiveness became a part of my day. It seemed I was either asking for it or doling some of it out; sometimes it was more one-sided than the other. With about six to seven hours a day in the saddle, there was much time to think. On the other hand, there were days when I wanted to quit thinking and just enjoy the beauty that surrounded me; so I did. Some issues I left alone, allowing time for them to achieve resolution. At other times efforts to resolve them seemed to make things worse; so, I decided that discounting my feelings was the best option. There were some days when I did not want to be a leader. I wanted to be comforted, to be told that everything was OK, to let someone else sweat the details, and to curl up and sleep through all distractions. That option was discounted immediately. Thankfully, Marion and Ruth had their estrogen sensors up and were so amazing in a couple of situations. They listened, offered hugs and kind words of encouragement. Girls just know what other girls need. Often Marion would make coffee for me while I soaked in the tub at the end of a long day. That simple act spoke to my heart.

We had many hours of fun, special memories and laughs on the journey. All in all, the team did very well in spite of the challenges along the way. Because these kinds of events are not easy, because of the challenge -- that is why we seek them out.

I will borrow the words from Theodore Roosevelt which sum up my feelings very well:

> *"Nothing in the world is worth having or worth doing unless it means effort, pain, difficulty... I have never in my life envied a human being who led an easy life. I have envied a great many people who led difficult lives and led them well."*

12

Stage Lights to
Disappointments

*"Acceptance of what has happened is the first step to
overcoming the consequences of any
misfortune."* (William James)

The fact that each team member was over the age of
forty three reminds me that every single one of us were well-
established in our characters before we dipped our wheels into
the Pacific Ocean. The way I dealt with the highs and lows of
this epic adventure had been cast long ago. My basic
personality was set in childhood and really has not changed
much. It was modified along the way, starting when I was
getting my first taste of the spotlight, and also of the darkness
of disappointment.

As a very young child my mom enrolled me in ballet
classes. I don't really recall how old I was but my first
experience on stage stands out vividly in my mind. There I
was on the front row, stage left with blinding lights in my eyes
and an elasticized circle of purple satin gracing my little face
and almond-shaped eyes. I was a "violet" dressed from head to
trunk in purple satin with sequins, a short, stiff tulle tutu and
pink tights. The lights were hot and I had a flock of butterflies

in my stomach. The elastic that held the twelve-inch circular purple satin "bloom" in place framed my forehead and went underneath my chin so that my face was exposed as the center of the flower. Did I mention how tight the elastic was? It felt like someone was strangling me.

I froze. All I remember beyond that was the overwhelming feeling that my breakfast was about to join me on stage. I felt hot, sweaty and claustrophobic and as if I were going to die. I have no idea if I danced or just stood there. No memory of collapsing, doing pliés, or twirling about -- nothing. I only recall the feeling that I could not wait to rip that head piece off and breathe again. My mom has a different story. As only a mother could recollect, I did perfectly fine.

Despite the case of stage fright a few years prior, with proper instruction and much patience from new dance teachers I was able to overcome that experience and learn some higher-level ballet skills. By the time I was eleven I had been promoted to pointe class and was selected to have a solo dance as a brown sparrow who -- interestingly -- ate the starch out of a Chinese woman's laundry bowl. For some reason the laundry lady was furious and she cut my character's tongue out. My dance was pretty enough to smooth over the storyline of a delicate creature that was mutilated in part. As a sixth grader, what we were playing out made no sense to me, but I loved the dance itself. It was graceful, dramatic and elegant. Later in that same recital, I was a snowflake that got to ice skate around the stage on pointe. That was one of my favorite dances, and I rehearsed it everywhere including in the foyer of Vestavia Elementary while I was on safety patrol after school. Obviously I was unsupervised and had little to do while waiting for the final buses to take the last children home from school, so I made the best use of time and flitted, fluttered and spun around the big open space.

It was beyond me that those who witnessed this delicate child dancing about in her own little world, catching imaginary snowflakes and getting lost in her own dream could see anything but a beautiful snow princess in her winter wonderland. Can you just imagine? Suddenly I was jolted from my fantasy snow world when I felt the burning of bewildered eyes on me. I quickly came back to reality and felt embarrassment wash over me like a crashing wave. When I sheepishly looked around I saw others watching me with smirks on their faces. No doubt those who were watching me were nonetheless impressed that I could be on safety patrol *and* dance simultaneously. Teachers, other students and even a parent or two snickered and walked away. I wanted to find a hole to crawl into. Even with that embarrassing experience, there was something that compelled me to dream and perform.

Just a few months later, Mom signed me up for a YMCA summer gymnastics camp. Coach Anne Mims paid special attention to me and had me doing back walkovers on the high beam by the end of the week. She told my mom that I "must" be on the team. My spine was so flexible that I could lie on my belly and fold both feet underneath my chin as my head touched my rear end. These were the days of Olga Korbut in the mid-1970's when acrobatics had just begun to morph into "real" gymnastics, so this flexibility was indeed a gift. With my dance background, it was a natural combination of talents to mesh into one.

Coach Anne was such a beautiful and sweet lady to me. I was completely eager to please her and do whatever she asked me to try. My zeal had taken over and I wanted to be the next Nadia. The dreamer came out again as I made up my Olympic gold-medal-winning routine in the den of my house. The performance ended abruptly as I tumbled into an end table, fracturing a growth plate in my right little toe. That deterred my workouts slightly but did not keep me from going to the National Guard Armory for gymnastics practice a few times a week. After all I was now on the competitive team and had goals of beating Nadia in the next Olympics. There was much work to be done.

Mom had signed me up for the Vannie Edwards Olympic Training Camp in the summer of 1978. A few months before this camp, I was eager to show a new skill that I had just learned. I shouted to Mom: "Watch this!" The trick was on the uneven parallel bars where I was to swing down from the high bar and literally wrap my body around the low bar at my hip joint. The intended movement was to place me on the low bar in a controlled fashion once I released the high bar and swung around the low bar backwards in a circle. Unfortunately, that did not happen. Instead, I landed in a cross-legged pile with my left elbow out of joint in such a grotesque manner that I screamed, "DON'T LOOK MOM!" This incident sent me directly to the emergency room and resulted in surgery to place two pins in my elbow.

As quickly as I could fall, there went my chances to attend the Olympic Training Camp and my shot at showing up Nadia in 1980. I was heartbroken. The initial injury ultimately required three operations and months of physical therapy. To this day my arm still has limited range of motion. However, that did not end my dream of going to compete in the 1984 Olympic Games. But they seemed so far off that I decided to put that on hold until I could at least move my arm again.

Dad was transferred to Fort Benning, Georgia, so it was time to move again. We left Tuscaloosa, the YMCA and the dance teacher who had brought the tongue-cut sparrow into my life. I was sad to leave but, as always before a move, Mom had prepared my brother, sister and me by showing us what opportunities there might be in the next city. This was our third time to Fort Benning so Columbus, Georgia was familiar ground. There were no gymnastics clubs and only one dance studio. However, my junior high school did have a new challenge for me -- the tumbling team. After tryouts I made the varsity team as a seventh grader. While some others could tumble, the skills attained at the YMCA catapulted me to a higher level. I suddenly became the star of the team and people who didn't know any better told me that I should go to the 1984 Olympics. My dream was rekindled.

In the eighth grade, gymnastics entrepreneur Bill Steele "discovered" my skills at a tumbling-team performance at the Salisbury Fair. He was preparing to open Gymnastics Plus, the first private gymnastics club in the area. Now maybe, just maybe, my dream could come true.

Hours and hours a week were spent in this indoor tennis facility that had been converted into a gym. With no heat or air conditioning, temperatures soared inside the gym during the hot summer months. It felt as if it was 100 degrees during our hours-long training sessions. I learned the value of hard work and perseverance. Suffice it to say that I grew in strength, stamina, skill and attitude. As I worked hard to excel on this gymnastics team, my name became known as one of the top gymnasts in the area. Could I *really* go to the Olympics? The Games were going to be in Los Angeles in 1984, the same summer I would graduate from high school. What dreams filled my head.

But something that occurred between eighth and ninth grades that ruined many dreams for my future. Some boy-related, early teenage experiences that I'll touch on later and that were beyond my ability to control caused me much grief for years. I was not emotionally able to cope with these issues and it was a real problem for me. We will never know what "couldda, shouldda, wouldda" happened, so it does no good to camp out in that line of thinking. These events caused great confusion and doubt in my mind of who I was, what I wanted, what I believed about myself. It seemed to me the best way to cope was through emotional eating and training ultra hard.

Between my freshman and sophomore years of high school, I gained twenty four pounds. I went from size 2 to size 14. It was such a sudden change that people asked me if I was

153

still doing gymnastics. At five-feet, three-inches tall, 144 pounds did not look very appealing, particularly in a leotard. My self-esteem was going nowhere but down. Eating disorders, such as anorexia and bulimia, were real problems in some clubs, and apparently my coaches knew better than to talk about a teenage girl's weight. So, while I knew I was heavy, I was also very strong and graceful, and I could carry my extra weight well. The nine years of ballet lessons helped me dance gracefully in between the tumbling passes. During this time I became angry and moody. When I performed, it seemed as if everything negative washed away and I was in my element. But the minute I stepped off the venue, that confident, graceful performer disappeared. I tried to cover up my emotions by acting tough and strong, but don't think I really did a very good job of it, in hindsight. As I got a little older I was able to mask my cares with a fake smile and convince many people that I had it all under control.

By my senior year of high school I won many all-around titles, set new school records, collected many accolades and even a partial scholarship to a small college in central Georgia. But the Olympics? Not a chance. It was time for Mary Lou Retton's dreams to become reality, not mine. I had bigger monsters in the closet to hide from.

Dreams of Days Gone By

At Georgia College for my freshman year, I had many normal college life experiences and some special ones as part of the gymnastics team. This was my first time away from home and I embraced the freedoms that followed suit. Being on the gymnastics team kept me grounded and away from most wild frat parties; our training was almost daily and our weekends took us to faraway places like Minot, North Dakota and Radford, Virginia. My dreams of competing on a grand scale were all but gone as I was just an average college gymnast from a tiny school in the National Association of Intercollegiate Athletics. I was too old and too big to do much in the sport other than coach.

Allowing myself to fall into another dream mode, I began to set my sights on being a wife and mother -- even though I had no viable candidates to help me attain either position. While I made good grades in general studies during that year of college, getting a degree quickly became something that I knew I did not really want to pursue. It was difficult for me to decide what I wanted to study: Physical Education? Nursing? Journalism? I could not decide. I squandered my parents' money and much of my time, trying to figure out what to do with my life. As sad as it is to admit, I simply did not value education. After all, I told myself, if I want to be a wife and mom, do I need a degree? I sold myself short.

Because of the painful events that happened before high school, which I will explain later, and the subsequent emotional scars I had from them, I began looking for approval from others. I had lots of girlfriends and a few guy friends. After a nasty break up with my high school boyfriend just before the end of my second quarter at Georgia College, I longed to feel loved and needed. At the time I was oblivious to it, but now that I am older and wiser I know that combination is toxic. Dropping out of college and making quite a few life-changing mistakes caused me to quit dreaming again for a time.

To be without vision and direction is a scary place for most -- if not all -- of us. During this two-year time of floundering came many more poor decisions. As most idealistic early-twenty-somethings feel, I was going to live forever. There were no real consequences to choices and I was immune to difficulties. The real problem was that I knew differently. The battle within my spirit of right versus wrong and self versus the world had become a full-scale war underneath my skin. I carried it privately, secretly wanting to just run away and hide from life.

I moved around a bit -- to the mountains of North Carolina, to northern New York State then back home with Mom and Dad. They offered too kindly to help me get back on the college track. I took them up on the offer for a year. It was there, at their lakefront home, that I began to dream again. By now I was 22 years old, but still not very grown up.

A few years went by with one breakup after another, and I began to dream of being a wife and mother. Why was this so important to me? Was it because my Mom had been such a superb example of it? Was this "dream" more of a fantasy, a form of escape? Surely it would resolve my need to be wanted and accepted by a man, wouldn't it?

At the age of 24, I found myself married and, all too quickly, a baby was on the way. Finally. My chance for another dream to take root. There was just a little drama with this however: He was on his way to Desert Storm and we had a shaky foundation from the beginning. We did not date nearly long enough, just a few short months, and we had very little in common. Since he was handsome and an Officer in the Army (like my Dad), I fell hard and fast. Note: Falling in love is never a good idea; try growing in love instead. Falling is painful.

He returned from war eleven months later to a baby and me. Within three months came a reduction in forces and he was out of the Army. We moved away from my parents and to Florida, near his parents. He went from job to job and spent time in between unemployed. I worked as a waitress then was hired by a nonprofit to be the House Mother at Serenity Shores, a home for homeless, pregnant women. That job just about did me in. Living in the home with four pregnant, homeless women, a husband and a toddler was not ideal for any of us. Eight months later, I resigned and took a position doing what I loved and knew well -- coaching gymnastics.

My then husband was having his own share of problems getting and keeping jobs. Another move back to Georgia promised a full-time, secure position for him during the day. I found a job as Team Director for the YMCA gymnastics team in the afternoon/evening hours. My son was born in the midst of this and it felt like the best opportunity to be able to raise children and to hold a job.

With three years of marriage behind us, a three year old and a three month old, he informed me that he "didn't love me, never had and never would." He said some other things to me that let me know he was serious, and that he had lost all hope in our marriage. I simply was not who he wanted as his wife.

Devastated to the core, I determined that I would make this man love me and prove him wrong. For years my mission became to earn his love and his affection. I was so desperate to make it happen that I lost all self-respect as a wife; my role as mother was the only fulfilling part of my life. The children loved me and filled many areas of my emotional needs; we had such wonderful relationships. I was a stay-at-home mom for the most part, or my part-time work would be in the afternoon/evenings when the kids would be with their father. How I thoroughly loved being a mother. But without fulfillment as a wife? It was just an incomplete dream. I was thankful for a few true girlfriends from church who were very helpful during these difficult years.

After eight years of trying unsuccessfully to win his heart and earn his love, my dream of being a wife came crashing down at last. I had done all I could. Marriage requires two people to be totally committed to the relationship's success and all hope was lost from my perspective. It was over. I was exhausted. Eleven years of marriage ended in divorce in 2001. So went the prized dream I had so carefully nurtured and crafted for most of my adult life -- or so I thought.

Deep within my soul is an unwritten but well-nourished desire to see great things happen. I don't know where this came from, but it is very real. Ever since I was a little thing I had big dreams, but one failure after another seemed to find me as I navigated my way into young adulthood. Only later would I realize the common denominator in each mistake -- me. This was a hard truth to admit, but if I were ever going to stop making stupid decisions, I had to take a close look at each failure and resolve to make some changes.

When dreams don't transpire many people give up. Not me; I am very determined (and a little stubborn.) I just dream another dream. After the failure of my marriage, I made a list of what I would look for should I happen to find myself in a relationship again. I decided that *if* there were a "dream man" out there, he would have to fit my list. I had very high expectations and he would have to be someone quite spectacular to be considered. Would you believe he was out there, and he did fit my "dream man" description? My list contained ten character traits and only two physical ones: blue eyes and dark hair.

BillyD and I first met in an unlikely place: an online Yahoo group called the "Divorced Christian's Chat Room." It was moderated by a Baptist preacher from Pennsylvania whose wife left him for another man. The church felt the need to release him from his duties and he started this group to encourage other Christians who have been hurt by divorce. It was not set up to be a dating website, so I felt safe going there to visit. Having been misunderstood by members of my own church who seemed more concerned about the divorce itself, rather than the many years of circumstances that led up to it, I did not feel very comfortable attending services there. So this chat room became a safe haven for me to hear a weekly sermon then have discussion with others about topics related to single parenting, judgment, moving on, etc. For several weeks I took note of what one seemingly intelligent man posted about. There were a few real strange cookies in the chat room, but this man was different. I kept my eye on his posts and thought, "Wow, he is really not like the others."

I was not ready to date. I was in nursing school and my children needed my attention in many ways. However, in my heart I longed to marry again at the right time and to the right person. I even prayed to be spared from the dating scene. That prayer was answered.

Weeks turned to months and one day, the chat room member I was watching posted a comment during a discussion about dating. "Billydisfree" was his screen name and he wrote: "I know what women want." That intrigued me so I sent him a private message for the first time. I asked, "Oh yeah? What is it that women want?" Little did I know, until much later, that he felt emboldened because he had just gone to see "What Women Want" (Mel Gibson) with a bachelor friend of his. He replied: "To be cherished. To be treated with tenderness. To be validated." That is what the movie taught him. My heart skipped at least three beats because this resonated with my soul. Was he real? I had to watch even more closely now, looking for inconsistencies or red flags.

His commitment to God spoke loudly to me. I could tell that he would be faithful as a friend, and one day as a husband – for some lucky lady. Over time, one by one, check marks were made beside my list of "musts" for my Dream Man.

This was back in the days of the early 2000s and meeting someone on the Internet was not as popular as it is today. We took our time, became good friends and decided to meet in person a full eight months after that initial private message. By that time we had exchanged phone numbers and pictures. From early on I could tell he was a candidate for the Tracy Dream Man School, but it was confirmed as time passed. The day his image came across my computer screen is one I will never forget: His bright smile was accentuated with beautiful dark blue eyes and brown hair.

We had our challenges after we met in person because we lived 400 miles apart. We had children to raise and careers to balance, so time together was limited to weekends when our children were with the other parent. In 2003, we decided it was time to let the kids meet and see how that went. Painstakingly, we waded through the waters of dating, growing in love and blending our two families together. It took a long time, but it was well worth it. Too many people rush into another marriage and the children are the ones who suffer. We were not about to put our kids through that again. My children and I moved to Florida in 2003 and, a few months later, BillyD proposed at Thanksgiving dinner, with four pairs of young eyes watching. It was magical and all six of us were so excited. My dream of being in a marriage where both parties were fully committed was coming true.

We married in 2004 and vowed to provide the best possible blended family that we could. With four children ages six through thirteen, we had our work cut out for us. Perhaps that is a whole book in itself. The point is: Don't sell yourself short on your dreams, ideas and hopes. Some things are worth the wait.

My dreams at that time became less about my desires and more about my new blended family. We had visions of family vacations, prayers at bedtime with each child, laughter at the kitchen table, being deeply loved by another and loving back equally. Our dream has come true with time, commitment, patience and hard work. I'm still living this dream and it is amazing.

When my daughter was just a tiny thing I would take her to visit my parents who lived about twenty miles away from town. There was a traditional farmhouse with a wraparound porch and three dormers that caught my eye as I drove to see Mimi and Papa. For a long time I admired that house, so beautifully set on a large piece of country farmland. One day I noticed the homeowner's name on the mailbox and wrote it down. "Why not give them a call and ask where they got their house plans?" I thought to myself. And that is just what I did.

The woman of the house graciously invited me, a complete stranger, to stop by one day so she could give me a copy of the plans. She did not invite me in but met me on that grandiose porch, flanked by huge hanging baskets that were full of giant ferns. She handed me photocopies of the actual pages of the book she found them in, complete with two pages of floor plans. I bade her farewell and thanked her kindly.

I was so excited that I drove right home and showed them to my then-husband. He looked at it and said, "Nice house, but we could never afford anything like that." I chose not to believe him and folded up the plans and put them in a book on the shelf for safe keeping. Years went by, dreams were dashed, life went on, most of my books were given away during quite a few moves when the children were young. The dream house was all but forgotten.

Fast forward to 2004, months before BillyD and I were to exchange vows. We felt strongly that each of our four children needed his or her own bedroom and space. We began looking for five-bedroom houses but they were out of our price range in town. We spent hours on the Internet and even visited the Mount Dora/Eustis area because housing was more affordable thirty miles out of Orlando. Nothing turned up. Time was ticking since we had a wedding date and needed a home of our own. His tiny three bedroom home wouldn't work and I was in an apartment. My lease was up the weekend of the wedding.

A few weeks passed. After almost giving up, we looked one more time on the Internet and found a Mount Dora real estate agents website advertising a country home. The picture was inviting. It showcased a large, wraparound porch, bay window and three dormers upstairs. Immediately, we looked up the address and went to see it for ourselves. The home was dated with country blue carpeting and light pink walls, but we could overlook that. Those are easy fixes. We found that we could enclose the loft and dining room to make it a five bedroom house. Huge oak trees dot the property. One had a low hanging branch that swooped down to the ground before taking itself back up in the air. It had a small orange grove in the yard. The next weekend we took the children to explore it, where each found at least one thing they especially liked about it. Yes, I could see raising our family here.

Something inside just felt "right." It was on the upper end of what we could afford but it was to be sold "as is" since it was in need of some work. When I got back to my apartment, I thought, "That house reminds me of my Alabama dream home. I wonder if I still have those plans from the early 1990s." As I looked at my scaled down library I whispered, "Lord, show me."

What were the chances of my finding those plans? The very first book I went to, I cautiously opened up. Tucked in between the first few pages were those two folded papers, now slightly discolored. The best part of this story is this - the plans are exactly the floor plans of the home we found near Mount Dora. That was all it took. I showed them to BillyD and he, too, knew it was meant to be.

13

Week Five: "Blood Highway"

Dyersburg, Tennessee to Amelia Island, Florida

"When we are motivated by goals that have deep meaning, by dreams that need completion, by pure love that needs expressing, then we truly live." (Greg Anderson)

Here we are - almost at the end of the journey. I felt a sense of relief mixed with a bit of hesitancy at this point. I was torn between wanting it to be over and hoping the mission would not end so quickly. Perhaps I was feeling a bit homesick? Coming back into the South where I have spent the majority of my life was refreshing and familiar.

In some ways I garnered security from the scenery of tall pine trees and multitudes of pickup trucks that surrounded us as we continued along the hilly roads. Southern drawls became more commonplace, and the sights and sounds of the South made me feel at home. We were on the homestretch and it was about time. I decided to just milk out all of the enjoyment I could because, once the Ride was over, I could not recapture any of it except for through memories. We had many more to make.

Day Twenty Nine / July 2, Wednesday
Dyersburg, TN to Savannah, TN
102.3 miles 3,209' climbing 6:07 saddle time 16.7 mph avg.
New Life Pentecostal Church, donated space

With a terrific rest day at a nice Holiday Inn Express, the team was ready to take on our dive into Dixieland. After spending so many nights on an air mattress in an open room, this particular hotel warmly welcomed us with granite countertops, friendly staff, an indoor pool, and a big bathtub. Oh how I loved being able to take a bath once I washed the road grit from my limbs. Our rooms seemed roomier, there was a laundry area just down the hall and the cleanliness of this hotel was worthy of a glowing TripAdvisor post.

We had a few hard days ahead of us due to the hilly terrain that Tennessee and Alabama had to offer. The summer heat of the South was expected to hit us full force with thick, hot air that was ripe with humidity known for exploding into daily afternoon thunderstorms. We also had some excitement to look forward to. We were mere days from being finished. We would soon talk about our mission on local Raycom Media television stations. My sister and brother-in-law were driving down from New York state so she could ride with us for two days.

July 2 started off with a newspaper interview and team photos in front of the hotel before we began our southeastward diagonal trek through Tennessee toward Alabama. We had a rather relaxing day of riding with little excitement or fantastic scenery. We would split up, regroup, split up and regroup. We knew by now that hilly terrain had that effect on us.

One meaningful encounter occurred as we were deep into Hardin County, Tennessee, not far from our day's destination. The sun was hot and our bodies glistened with sweat. The rolling hills and curvy roads were fun to ride. Ruth, Bill and I were pedaling along a country road when a man on

164

the side of the road waved us down and offered us bottled water. A few yards away was his wife, digging more ice-cold bottles of water out of a cooler in the trunk of their car. There were no other houses, no other people. Just the five of us on the road at that point in time. Feeling very much like a bike racer being handed water at a feed zone, I smiled hugely and shouted: "Thank you so much!" as Bill and I zoomed by on a slight downhill. He showed his appreciation for the ice-cold liquid as well. Ruth, being the genteel, beautiful person that she is, had stopped to talk with the couple. They told her that they had passed us a few miles back. Knowing there was no other way for us to go except past their house, they rushed home to fill the cooler with ice and water and waited for us to come by. Yes, we were indeed in the South. They manned their self-appointed aid station until the entire team had passed: Southern hospitality at its best. We were refreshed in mind and body.

As we came to Savannah, Tennessee, we crossed over the Tennessee River. What a lovely river it is etched between two steep banks and lined with rich, full trees. Unlike the Mississippi, this river was a pretty shade of deep blue on that day. Rachel, Director of Hardin County Convention and Visitors Bureau, asked us to stop at the Tennessee River Museum, where she would have snacks for us. Bill, Ruth and I stopped for a very nice little visit. Somehow the others missed the museum and went on to find a place to eat lunch; so the three of us got our fill of trail mix, bananas, cheese sticks and juice. On the front steps of the museum, Billy, Ruth and I posed for a photo for the local newspaper. We then headed to the church, which would be our home for the night to find the others had arrived just ahead of us.

New Life Pentecostal Church hosted us in the upstairs Youth Center and invited us to dine with them at their weekly Wednesday night supper. They were very gracious. We showered, relaxed and began to plot our next day's route into northwestern Alabama. Dinner time was 6pm and we were more than ready for it when it became time. The entire meal was home cooked, full of flavor and southern lovin'. Chicken, roast beef, potatoes, green beans, several salads and desserts - oh, there were so many to choose from. It is possible that we put on two pounds each in this very short timeframe. Conversation over supper was about how we were going to get out of town and into Alabama. The locals inquired of our plans, so we obliged.

- *"That road's called Blood Highway. Are you sure you wanna take it?"*
- *"You're crazy to take that road. People get killed on that road all the time."*
- *"I wouldn't do it if I were you. You have to go another way."*

Church members tried their best to dissuade us from taking a short highway to the Alabama line that we had made our route. It was only twenty five miles to the line before the road opened up and became much wider. There really was no other choice without adding many more miles and changing our route. Still, it made for falling asleep a bit treacherous as I reflected on our last experience in Wichita when we refused to take the advice of locals. We had to make a decision and feel good about it. A good night's sleep should help us think better.

Day Thirty / July 3, Thursday
Savannah, TN to Cullman, AL
118.7 miles 4,321' climbing 6:24 saddle time 18.5 mph avg.
Days Inn, discounted rate

Over coffee and a bowl of cereal in the church fellowship hall, we decided that we would take the scheduled route and that Clay would shadow us in the SAG when dangerous curves were in our path. There would be hills in the first few miles, so we knew we would split up. The plan was to regroup at the Alabama State Line. As Divine intervention showed itself yet again on this ride, a cool front dropped the temperatures about ten degrees and we had beautiful weather for riding. Skies were blue and crisp and it felt more like late September than July. Following a quick stop for a team photo, we entered Alabama and Keith, Ruth and Bill were off. We had survived Blood Highway without incident. Whew.

Before too long, however, Clay was flagging us down to tell us that a reporter was trying to find us for an interview. She had found Ed and Marion as they stopped to repair a flat along Highway 20. Then she called Clay, who arranged for us all to meet at a McDonald's for the interview. When she got to us she told me that her boss was told by the head honcho at Raycom Media to "Find that team and get the story!" This "big boss" happens to sit on the board of directors at Hope for the Warriors. He had heard long before that we would be passing through his town and determined to make good on his promise to share our story. Perhaps it was the dramatic pursuit of the news reporter that made this interview such a good one. Or could it have been that her questions led to personal, touching answers from the team member she spoke with? It became a two-minute story on the news that night, and we got a copy of it. This was our first television interview and it was exciting.

Upon rolling into Cullman we quickly found a Wendy's, where a reporter would be waiting for us, according to Clay. The Dairy Queen was just a bit ahead of us so we agreed to stop and get Frosties; of course they hit the spot. Temperatures that day were in the high eighties and the hot, summer sun was glaring. From there we headed straight to the hotel where a dear friend's sister made arrangements for us to stay with a big discount. We all headed straight for the outdoor pool after checking in and putting our bike in our rooms. Some of us kept our cycling gear on and dove right in, and had a good time for a while. I took a funny video on my phone of

Clay harassing some other team members in the water while, unbeknownst to him, Scott stealthily snuck up behind him and uprooted him, causing him to be dragged underwater. What was so great was that Clay is our biggest team member and Scott is the smallest. We all got a great laugh out of that. A bit later we piled into the SUV and, with Scott and me taking our usual place in the very back, headed to Cracker Barrel to meet my sister and her husband for dinner. We took up a large table, enjoyed a huge meal then took pictures outside in the rocking chairs on the front porch of the restaurant. What a nice way to end a long day. My plate of hot, buttery, pecan pancakes tasted so good.

Day Thirty One / July 4, Friday
Cullman, AL to Oxford, AL
93.9 miles 4,026' climbing 5:09 saddle time 18.1 mph avg.
Courtyard Marriott, Oxford, compliments of Robin Kelleher, personal donation

Happy Birthday USA! It was July 4 and we had a lot on tap. My sister, Leigh, and her husband met us at our hotel that morning. He drove her over and he was going to meet with some other family members instead of ride with us. Our parents were set to meet us in Oxford and BillyD would return later in the day to see us through till the end. Leigh is a very strong rider and supporter of our cause so we were really looking forward to her being a part of the team for this segment. She even flew me up to her house in May, prior to the ride, to have a fundraiser for Hope for the Warriors. I was really excited about sharing this experience with her and our other family members.

The day played out as follows: We loaded the trailer and fueled our bodies, then met Leigh in the parking lot before we had to roll. My rear tire had decided it had enough and flattened while I slept that night. I had to do a quick tire change. One team member kept muttering under his breath,

"Time to go" and making reference to "daylight is burning." It
wasn't even 7 am yet and my patience wore out primarily
because I did not like his impatience and pressure. What was
the big deal? We hadn't even yet read our daily story from
Hope for the Warriors. Very sweetly, Ruth said, "It's seven."
Feeling enormous pressure from several sources, I quickly bit
her head off. In a curt tone I stated: "Does it look like we are
all ready to go? What is the hurry? " or something to that
effect. My brother-in-law's eyes met mine and I suddenly felt
sheepish. At this point I cannot even remember if we read a
story that morning or if we just started rolling. The stress of
the situation dissipated rather quickly. I apologized to Ruth for
being snappy. She graciously accepted, saying that she
understood. I realized, too, that her gentle reminder of the time
wasn't internally motivated.

The hills came early and lasted some forty miles as
we made our way south and east to Oxford, Alabama. The
group splintered a bit, as expected, and Leigh and I rode side
by side, catching up with each other. I specifically chose this
route because my family previously lived in nearby Anniston,
where my brother was born and I was a toddler while Daddy
was in Vietnam. My mother's parents lived in the tiny town of
Lineville, which we would pass through the next day. Hearing
my mom speak warmly of this area of the country made me
want to pay it a little visit. I had not been in the area since my
grandmother's funeral in 1990. This part of the route would be
a time for reflection as we neared the end of the mission. It felt
a bit like I was coming full circle, as I had hoped. Leigh and I
had a great time riding and chatting. I remembered feeling so
jealous of her as a sibling, but now that we had grown up,
those feelings had passed. We are able to be friends.

In one of the bigger cities that we came through,
traffic was heavy on a four-lane road. At a traffic light, a
policeman told one of our teammates that he would block for
us and that we could take the entire lane. An impromptu escort

-- how about that? He supported us from the rear for several miles and we were grateful indeed. Once we got out of the city, he pulled up beside us, waved us on and smiled widely, knowing he had been a help to us. Again, Southern hospitality showed itself to our team. We soon rounded a curve as we came into Anniston's flag-lined roads. Seeing the wind blow hundreds of Old Glories just made my heart sing. A tidal wave of patriotism flooded my soul and tears again filled my eyes with pride over the beauty of our nation's flag and what it represents. How many lives have been wounded or lost as it flew overhead in battlefields around the world?

Just days earlier when we were back in Augusta, Kansas at Mayor William's house, I took a phone call from Curtis, a firefighter from Oxford, Alabama. He had heard our story and knew we were coming to his town. He asked if he could arrange a fire truck to escort us into Oxford on July 4. And here we were on Independence Day -- and the big, red escort was waiting for us. This was a very cool way to make an entrance into town. Scott and I were like little kids chasing down the truck while the team held back a little bit behind us. We were none too worried about it as emotion took over; the others were about thirty feet back. Motorists looked a little surprised to see us tailing the big red rig as we legally blew through red lights. Curtis, our fireman driver, led us directly to our hotel where my parents, brother-in-law and BillyD were waiting. It was a fantastic way to end our ride for the day. But much more lie ahead for us, as it was still early afternoon.

I had been contacted by the Captain Kyle Comfort Foundation, which raises money to support our service members who were wounded in action and also families of those killed in action. Joel Denney and his wife Nancy met us at the hotel and presented our team with a gift card for dinner and supplies along the way. Having served in the US military themselves, this thoughtful couple continue to serve other military causes through the foundation. We were touched and grateful for their support. The work they do through this particular foundation is truly wonderful. Their kylecomfortfoundation.org website is an inspiration.

Joel and I have kept in touch since our Big Ride and he shared with me his insights to how he interprets Live It on a daily basis:

> *"I am retired, thus the only thing of value I have to offer is my time. I am willing to share my time with just about anyone who can use it effectively. So if I have a dream it is to help others fulfill their dreams, reach their potential and position them to be successful in their faith, life, family, work and play. I give most of my time to two Foundations. The first supports service members and their families in time of extreme difficulty occasioned by loss of life or serious injury while in service to our country. The second is one that undertakes construction projects to support families in need of one of the single most essential element to raising and stabilizing a family -- a home -- we build homes. It is these two plus working with Carpenter's for Christ building churches from time to time that give me the most satisfaction. So my one dream is real and still being realized -- my dream is to help others!"*

Joel and Nancy are beautiful examples of doing what they love while helping others.

At our day's destination in Oxford, the team checked into the hotel on that warm, muggy Independence Day and had a few minutes to relax. We then made plans to have dinner. It was fun to have several of my family members with us and we had one big, very hungry group.

As fate would have it, a Mellow Mushroom was within walking distance of our hotel and was fully decorated in a cycling theme. The owner is a bicycle fanatic, just like our team. It was an easy decision where to have dinner. Thanks to Clay and his exuberance for our mission, Mellow gave us a 25

percent discount off for our team meal. We had a fun time
snapping photos, filling up on calzone, pizza and other calorie-
packed food and drinks. Filled to the brim, most of our party
decided that going out for the city-wide firework celebration
would be too much and opted to go back to the hotel for a
good night's rest. However, BillyD, Scott and I were up for
more adventure, so we made the short drive to the big lake for
the rest of the celebration.

Our firefighter friend invited us to sit with his family
in a special section very close to where the fireworks were
launched. We had a front row seat to an amazing show. Once
the finale had given its final burst, the three of us wearily
walked a mile or so to the car and quietly drove back to the
hotel. We knew we had another long day awaiting us, now just
about seven hours away. Before getting into bed, I took one
last look over the route for the morning and was very much
unsettled by it. Trepidation seeped into my mind and I just
could not take our team on the route that Ed had changed. As
has happened several times on this trip, Ed told me that when
he uploaded the routes from Map My Ride to Ride With GPS,
the new mapping system took the shortest route possible. The
original route kept us away from Highway 431 south because
of the dangers the highway held. The four-lane road was used
by logging and poultry trucks and is a major thoroughfare with
little-to-no shoulder at times. It has low visibility at times and
very high traffic. Friends of mine from an Alabama cycling
club warned us not to take it. Since this warning came from
cyclists, I felt that we should heed it. Even though it was
shorter and might have saved us time, Highway 431 was
known by locals as being risky and it did not seem like the
best option.

Since our group split up after dinner, we did not go
over the route as a team, which we should have. By the time
we got in from fireworks, everyone else had retired for the
night. I stayed up a while longer, looking back at the original

route I outlined over a year ago and sent out an email to the sleeping team members that we had to make a change. I knew that the others would get the message and have time to update their Garmins, and felt like I had made the right call. Now it was time to get some sleep; I had about six hours left before Day 32.

As my head hit the soft pillow, I thought: "What a wonderful way to spend the day celebrating the freedom we have. The freedom to travel, to worship, to speak openly ... to get to ride our bikes and raise awareness for those who have sacrificed their all to protect our freedoms is beyond living a dream."

A deep sleep came over my weary body in mere seconds. We had a long day ahead of us, perhaps the most climbing of the entire trip.

Day Thirty Two/ July 5, Saturday
Oxford, AL to Columbus, GA
121.8 miles 7,333' climbing* 7:52 saddle time 15.5 mph avg.
* Our biggest climbing day on the trip came in Alabama, not the Rockies
Holiday Inn Express, compliments of First Baptist Church, Columbus

The story from this day is described in the next chapter, "Doubts," so I will not recount it here. Suffice it to say, that it was not the best day for our team and I was embarrassed that my family was there and a part of it. My daughter and her boyfriend paid a surprise visit as well. How my sister and I got separated was a gaffe, but mistakes were made by several on that day -- including me. We all felt the stress of not only a long day, but a long journey. I believe it is safe to say that we were all looking forward to completing the ride. There were just three days and about 300 more miles to go. It was still too soon to give up mentally. At the end of the ride that day, we decided to cut each other some slack;

everyone deserved a break.

There were two people waiting for me when I got to the hotel: Steve Bartomioli, Team Director of Hope for the Warriors and Catherine Bradshaw, a nurse who worked with injured service members at Fort Benning's War Transition Unit. She had arranged for four wounded warriors to ride with us the next morning and it was important for me to meet with her. Steve had come to support us all the way to the end so we had things to review. However, I was torn because Leigh was still out there somewhere. Thankfully I knew she was with Marion and Ed and that Ed was carrying a GPS monitor. But Clay was not with them, and they had no SAG to help them along. I had to trust that they were fine and would be able to stop at stores for their nutrition/drink needs, just as Scott and I did most of the afternoon while the two of us rode on our own.

After I showered, I met with Steve and Catherine. About two hours later, as the sun sank lower on the horizon, Marion rolled up with a huge smile on her face and a watermelon tucked beneath her arm. Leigh had arrived safely and my family all went to greet her. As it turned out, they never got to meet up with Clay and she rode for more than half her journey with only a Snickers bar for nourishment. With Clay always available, some did not carry cash because he was a phone call away. However, phone service was poor in eastern Alabama and Ed's battery had died. Those two misfortunes, plus the fact that Clay was on a different road altogether, made for a challenging afternoon for them. The change in the route was the main cause for blame, but miscommunication and drained batteries only made it worse.

Our Randonneuring training was quite helpful in this instance. While on those rides, we had no SAG. It was incumbent on each rider to provide his/her own supplies and to work with the cards dealt them. Nevertheless, isn't that how life is? We are all dealt cards. Some are tough hands to play, some come easier. What about the cards dealt to our military?

Surely their missions do not always go according to plan.
Injuries come out of the blue. Trauma forces itself into
someone's unsuspecting life. Their entire world turns upside
down ... and these players are left to make the best of the hand
that they are given.

Our most challenging day was full of climbing
emotional and physical mountains. It was a day when each
team member had to reach deep within to find strength to
press on. Our fortitude was tested -- and we all passed. While
we could each rest well that night knowing that the hardest
days were now finally behind us, I wondered how were our
fellow citizens, the defenders of our freedom able to cope with
their difficult days? What we endured was over in a matter of
hours, a mere bump in the road as compared to the challenges
of the wounds these brave veterans suffer. Where do some get
the resolve to rebuild their lives? Many do not. Many cannot
without help.

Day Thirty Three / July 6, Sunday
Columbus, GA to Albany, GA
87.4 miles 2,552' climbing 5:24 saddle time 16.2 mph avg.
Sherwood Baptist Church, donated space and the Sceals
household

Because our family moved to Columbus, Georgia
during my formative year in the seventh-grade, I typically say
I was raised there. For about a dozen years, starting at age
twelve, I even called it "home." Dad retired at Fort Benning on
July 1, 1982. I graduated from Shaw High School in 1984,
attended Columbus State University, got married and had my
first child at Martin Army Hospital on Fort Benning. Since it
really didn't inconvenience anyone, it just seemed right to
route us through the closest thing to my hometown.

After breakfast and loading the trailer, we rode a
short distance to the National Infantry Museum at Fort

Benning where we met a television reporter and four guest riders scheduled to join us. Dad had served his final assignment at the Infantry School, supervising the writing of the initial field manuals that described how enlisted infantrymen are to perform their Military Occupational Specialty duties. The recently completed museum and adjoining grounds evoked strong feelings of pride and appreciation. It is a grandiose structure with a huge statue at its entrance. As we waited for the reporter to arrive, I stood at the base of the giant structure and read the accompanying inscription. Suddenly, as I looked up, I pictured my father's face on that statue, and became so proud of how he spent twenty six years of his life in service to our great nation. I shuddered in that eerie and overwhelming moment.

Soon the television reporter showed up for the interview. One of the questions she asked was: "How has this ride changed your life? " Being caught off guard by this question, my blunt and honest answer was, "It's too soon to tell!" I knew that it would, but was not quite sure how to verbalize it yet. There was still more to come. As I write with several months to unpackage all that transpired, I have a better answer. It is not yet time to divulge that information.

Our team spent a few minutes of time amid the beautiful memorials that grace the meticulously landscaped grounds of the Infantry Museum's property. These few minutes to survey the grounds as the reporter interviewed the wounded warriors who came to meet us, were clearly not enough to pay any meaningful tribute to the countless number of lives represented there.

The team was blessed to spend a little time chatting with each of those wounded soldiers who joined us at Benning. I was touched by their stories. One gentleman told us cycling had saved his life. Another told me of the horrors of living with post traumatic stress and how cycling had given her something to help her get her mind off of the things that haunt her. How I wish we had days to ride with them, but it could be only for a few short miles. As we exited Fort Benning, we bade them farewell and good luck, hoping to have offered them some encouragement. We were the ones, however, who rode off encouraged.

Before long it was time to get on the road and continue our eastward trek. Another state down. Only Georgia and Florida to go. We had a rather gentle ride down a highway that I had spent thousands of miles on when I was a young mother. The road between Albany, Georgia and Columbus held more memories for me and the quiet hours of riding them today were bittersweet. We passed the convenience store in Richland where I used to have to meet my ex to swap the kids for the weekend. I cried quietly as we rode past. Later on we went by a store where I had a spitball fight in the car with my very young children over a dozen years ago. I smiled and even laughed a little as we pedaled by there. A bit further up the road we went right by a friend's country farmhouse where I had spent time while secretly wishing I could have an old homestead like her's one day. Such rich recollections. The team had no idea that I was taking a ride down memory lane, nor did they need to. This part of the journey was a private time for healing from my own scars and battles in life.

Several years ago, I befriended a Category 1 racer from Albany who organized and ran a cycling team with her husband. The team was a competitive element of the Pecan City Pedalers, a local cycling club in that area. A year before we were due to pass through town, I asked if they would like to meet us and escort us into Albany. They were happy to oblige. Thirty miles out of town, we began seeing spandex-clad riders in orange just ahead. There at the appointed meeting place were about twenty five or so Pedalers waiting for us. I was so happy to see Michele and her husband, Kent, again. We hugged, filled bottles, introduced everyone and began the short trek to our host town for the night. Taking beautiful, mostly flat country roads through fields of who knows what, we enjoyed a relaxed rolling pace and chatted our way into town.

Another dear friend of mine from my years in Albany is Diane. We had children who were the same age and spent many hours together while we had play dates. She had made arrangements for our team to stay in homes of some of the townspeople. We rolled into our final meeting place for the day, Sherwood Baptist Church, to a small crowd of cheering, flag-waving people. I recognized most of the faces since I had spent eight years of my life in Albany while I reared my young children. Again, bittersweet memories came to mind.

While another television news reporter waited patiently for our team to arrive, I thanked the Pecan City Pedalers group and endured the southwest Georgia gnats that had come to greet us by the thousands. A few of us contributed to the interview, while the others rode about five blocks to the local Dairy Queen.

Diane had arranged for us to stay in three different houses; however, the team wanted to pack into one house in order to make logistical preparations for the next morning easier. BillyD and I stayed with a couple that had been my friends over a decade before. Thanks to Sherwood Church, the team stayed at one of the church's missionary houses. BillyD and I got a much-needed dinner date together. Our hosts, the Sceals, were delightful and we stayed up quite late visiting with them. It was terrific to reconnect with them, but I felt a little bad for not being there with the team. While it felt odd to be separated from them, the mission house was not big enough for all of us.

We have one full day of riding left, then a short day. .... And it would be over. Was I ready? There was no time to reflect; by now we were quite set in our ways of ride, clean up, eat, write a blog, go to bed, repeat.

Day Thirty Four / July 7, Monday
Albany, GA to Waycross, GA
118.6 miles 1,795' climbing 6:16 saddle time 18.9 mph avg.
Best Western Hotel

Ahead of us we had over 100 miles of farmland to view as we rolled due east for one more day in the heat of July. The cold front was long gone, and we felt the stifling humidity of southwest Georgia in the throes of summertime. At times the heaviness of the air made it a bit hard to breathe. But the hills became more like small, gentle rollers which was advantageous to us. Our legs were heavy from yesterday's ride. We could pedal in a paceline and enjoy some rest time today.

For the first ten miles or so we had two sheriff deputies escort us on the bypass and the main highway in Tifton, Georgia. They missed us initially but quickly caught us and hemmed us in on the bypass giving us the entire lane. One more time we heard some honks and heard a few accolades shouted our way as the journey was nearing an end. We passed very close by the Marine Corps Logistics Base and the Miller Brewery as we exited the eastern part of Albany. There were familiar landmarks to me from when I spent time in Albany between 1994-2002. As we wheeled away, I left behind the worst of the memories of time spent there. I choose to recall the many ones that were so sweet and the few deep friendships that continue to grow. Leaving the past behind allowed me to refocus on what a beautiful family that BillyD and I have built together. With adversity as a teacher, we can now appreciate the good things in life that we could otherwise take for granted.

Forty-five miles down the way we saw a cute, young and ever-so-slight woman snapping photos of us on the highway. She wore a very bright blue sleeveless top and what looked like credentials on a lanyard hanging around her neck. We smiled and waved but she made no effort to stop us. A few

miles later as we got closer to Tifton we spotted two old
school buses with the rear three-quarters of the roof sliced off,
as if they were some redneck versions of a pickup truck. There
were mounds of green in the back. What could it be? With
hilarious delight, Marion called out "LOOK! It's a watermelon
truck! We don't have those in the Netherlands!" Scott, Ed, and
I laughed and took photos of these improvised haulers. Three
of our other teammates had gone ahead, apparently in a hurry
to escape the heat and dive into the pool awaiting us at our
hotel in Waycross.

   Within minutes, the mystery lady in blue was on the
right side of the road ahead of us and wildly waving us down.
We pulled into the parking lot where she had hastily parked
and said in her delicate high-pitched southern drawl: "Hey!
The others said that you were the ones to talk to. Do you have
a moment for a photo and an interview? I'm with the Tifton
Gazette." We were happy to accommodate her request right
there on the side of GA Highway 82 East. We made great time
getting to Waycross, and it was so good to have time to relax
for a few hours before dinner. BillyD was there waiting for me
with the air conditioner on high and coffee brewing. While
that was great, what I really longed for was a nice, warm bath
and a nap. After a bit of wind-down time, I went to have
dinner with the team and found that quite a few of our friends
had driven up from Florida to escort us home the next day. I
was exhausted and not very hungry but still appreciated the
effort that our friends had made, so I tried to be gracious. After
several people asked, "Are you OK? " I realized that my acting
had not been academy award material. What I really needed
was a good night's sleep, which is just what I got very soon
after dinner. I'm sure that I was not the only one who felt worn
down; it showed in the eyes of a few others as well. Despite
being fatigued, a spark of excitement flickered within me as I
tried to imagine our beach-side homecoming.

Day Thirty Five / July 8, Tuesday – Final Day!
Waycross, GA to Amelia Island, FL
75.9 miles 486' climbing 3:57 saddle time 19.2 mph avg.
Days Inn, discounted rate

I awoke with mixed feelings. Could this be the day we had longed for? Was it actually going to be over? How was it going to feel to have the wetness of the salty ocean water between my toes? In some ways it all happened so fast. In other ways, the days and weeks dragged on. The clash that followed us off and on since Wolf Creek Pass seemed to flare up, causing frustration and discomfort. But as a team, we were determined to accomplish our mission. Yes, we were ready and YES, we were going to finish on time and according to plan. Nothing short of a catastrophic event could thwart our final day. My dream of propelling my bike across our homeland and our team mission to support Hope was too important to allow weariness or disappointments to interfere.

Seventy-seven more flat miles is all that was in between us and the Atlantic Ocean. Blinding orange rays of sunrise pierced the shadows from the hotel's three floors.The skies were clear, the air again heavy with southeast Georgia humidity. Despite a bit of road noise from the highway in front of the hotel, all bystanders were poised to listen to the touching story. There was magic in the air and emotion on the faces of the group members. Hope for the Warriors saved the best, most compelling story for last. Steve Barto read it moments before we rolled out for our last day on the road. There were about fifteen of us who heard the impact that our ride's beneficiary, Hope, has made on so many lives. This is the final story provided by Hope to inspire us for our last day on the road.

A note from Sergeant Major Brad Kasal

Sgt. Maj. Kasal is a highly decorated Marine now

immortalized in the monument No Man Left Behind that Hope For The Warriors unveiled last year. He could not attend, but wrote this inspiring letter:

To all in attendance, I first must say I apologize for not being able to attend in person. My deepest regrets as I'm unable to get away from my current duties. But I do want to take this time and write a few words to say thank you to all in the Hope For The Warriors organization. Thank you for what you do for all our nation's service members, most specifically our wounded. It's remarkable to know our young Americans who have raised their right hand and volunteered to support and defend this great nation, are never forgotten. That there are great Americans taking care of fellow great Americans. This is what makes our Country unique and special. This is the American spirit and the American way.

People are the US Armed forces greatest asset, and two of those great Americans are in attendance today. While there are three individuals depicted in the statue you see before you, I can assure you I was nothing more than an unlucky individual who was fortunate to be surrounded by many of the greatest of our generation. In this particular case I had one on both flanks of me by the names of then LCpl Dane Shaffer and Chris Marquez. The date of Nov 13th, 2004 was a day that brought many unfortunate casualties. However it was also a day when young Americans showed what they were made of and displayed extraordinary spirit and heroism.

I remember vividly as I lay wounded inside the house that day, two young Marines who suddenly appeared at my side. They did so after running across an open room covered by deadly automatic weapons fire. The thing that first caught my attention, besides that they were crazy, was neither Marine carried a weapon. They left them behind, so they would have their hands free in order to more capably carry me to freedom. First, this displayed the trust they had in their fellow Marines who were assigned the task of

covering them as they crossed the open room unarmed. There was only one way out, and that was back through the same killzone that already caused several Marines to be wounded. They ended up crossing that kill zone four times, each time unarmed, and each time trusting their fellow Marines.
They did it because they were Marines. And that's just what Marines do.
To the Marquez and Shaffer families, if you are in attendance, you should be very proud. If we ever ask where we get such fine men, we only have to look as far as their family.
We as a nation should never forget men like these two and all the others who serve today in one of our nation's most trying times. They are truly incredible Americans and it was my honor to serve beside them
Again, I want to say thank you and God Bless.

With that kind of inspiration we began our final push to the ocean. At first we were all quiet, perhaps in reflection or due to the early morning hour and lack of coffee. Either way, it was fine with me because I was still processing that story, imagining what war must be like, picturing that bronze statue depicting two Marines carrying one of their own to safety, bravely unconcerned for their own. My mind wondered where these men are today and what their lives are like. The statue now stands as a reminder that in war, no man is to be left behind. It is placed at Camp LeJeune, North Carolina where the many injured warriors recover. Camp Pendleton (California) is home to a second tribute statue that was unveiled more recently with great fanfare to serve as a reminder of the same truth at another base where many injured warriors return.

The day's plan was to stop at the Florida State Line

for photos, then have just one more short stop for a phone call to coordinate activities at the beach. A week after Pam left us in Arizona, she called and told me that she was planning a party for us at the hotel after we had our ocean-side ceremony. As a fitting surprise, she had also arranged a final police escort from the causeway to the beach.

It was a sunny day with temperatures forecast for the low 90s as highs. As we rode at more than 20 mph, the wind cooled us as it passed over our sweaty skin. It is when we stopped that our bodies felt the heat. Overhead there were typical summer clouds that morph into various animal shapes in the sky. Along with taking note of them, and sensing their welcoming us back to our home territory, I began to get excited by seeing Florida scrub oaks, palmettos and Spanish moss in the trees. Our friends who joined us asked great questions as we rode in a beautiful double paceline along low-traffic roads. Questions like: "So what was your favorite thing about this? " "How hard was it? " "What are you going to miss about this when it is over? " and the like. There was much excitement in the air, and the cares of the previous weeks seemed to disappear. At mile 26 we crossed the St. Mary's River bridge and into Florida. Only fifty one miles to go. That translated to just a bit over two hours; we were going to make our noontime appointment with family and friends and have minutes to spare.

The next thirty five miles went by very quickly. With such a big bunch of people riding in a double paceline, rotating through and enjoying ourselves, we were making great time. The wind was a non-issue; everyone was chatty and excited. We made the call to confirm our arrival time and everything was now in place.
Fifteen miles to go... eight miles to go.....

We started getting into formation -- shortest to tallest, side by side. Our friends gave us a bit of space so that the team could get the glory of riding over the final causeway and into the beach parking lot together. With Steve Barto graciously driving SAG, Clay rode in with us. This was our order from left to right, front to back, in a double paceline: Tracy and Scott, Ruth and Marion, Bill and Keith, Clay and Ed. Two by two and we looked absolutely fantastic. Just as we had gotten into our places and crossed the causeway, we spotted our final police escort waiting for us. He sounded his siren, pulled in front of us, and led us about three miles to the beach.

Marion said aloud, "Tracy -- in case I get too caught up in all of the excitement at the beach, I want to thank you now for inviting me to be a part of this experience!" Scott, Bill and Ruth chimed in and a lump the size of my fist rose in my throat. I took a deep breath and through a big smile, came words to Ruth that it isn't yet time for tears. Marion's gratitude was filed away in my heart, and I recall feeling so proud of her in particular. Anyone who knows Marion knows that she has some incredible drive, however, at the start of this endeavor, she proclaimed herself as the weakest link. She began this journey with some extra weight on her-- but not anymore. It was a joy to witness her transformation into a fully confident cyclist. The Marion I thought I saw long before this trip surfaced along the way.

After a right turn, we saw that straight ahead there was a clearing as the vista widened. That could only mean one thing: The ocean was straight ahead. Again, emotion choked up into my throat, but I forced it down with a big gulp. It was not yet time for tears as I had to be able to see where I was going; tears would just get in the way. Trying to take it all in was surreal, mostly impossible for me. But to live in this moment of success was astounding. I recall thinking: "Wow, no century ride tomorrow; what will I do with my time? " While it was wonderful to have arrived, there was also a little anxiety thrown in the mix. How would my life change after the Ride?

Just a few blocks ahead I could see a crowd with

posters, flags and signs a waving. Cowbells were ringing, cheers filled the air as we rolled closer, closer. The police escort with his lights whirling got us to the cul de sac then peeled off, leaving us eye to eye with our supporters who had come to welcome us. Out of almost uncontainable excitement I bunny-hopped my bike, gaining a whopping two inches between Goldilox and the pavement. Several of us fist-pumped the sky in jubilation. Cheers and whistles came from the crowd of a couple of dozen friends and family members.

There I saw BillyD, my parents and Ricky on the edge of the crown. Scores of others: spouses of teammates, cycling friends from Orlando, Pam, Anne Marie, Kenny, Fred, siblings of other riders, co-workers, TJ (the little boy who had been sending pictures to us) and his mom, Scott's parents, his son and so many more who had come out to welcome us back to Florida. The fact that these people would give up a work day and drive a few hours to cheer us was such a treat. Of course, at noontime in July, there were regular beach-goers who had no idea why their beach time had just been interrupted by such a crowd.

Quick hugs and high fives were shared but we were not stopping. No way, we were too close. We were not yet to the water. The air smelled of salt and oceanic aromas. The warm breeze carried the sounds of being on shore. The team removed helmets and bike shoes but all the while in forward motion as we were drawn to the edge of the lapping surf. This is what we waited for. This was the end of the journey. I was so caught up in the moment of "being done" that Bill had to slow me down to wait on the others. He said, "Wait, Tracy. Aren't we all going to walk together to the water? " Good idea. Settle down, Trace.

Within seconds we were all lined up and rolling our bikes to the white foamy ever-moving edge of the Atlantic Ocean to dip our front wheels in to finally, completely, officially finish the journey. I let out a shout of victory and held my beloved Goldilox up overhead in complete domination of more than 3,000 miles of road that passed underneath my wheels. I looked down at my sleekly toned legs that had been kissed by the sun for five weeks and was so grateful for a job well done. The pain in my back had subsided -- or was it the endorphins that masked it? All of our bodies, with bumps, bruises and aches, had performed better than we imagined. The wide smile that took over my suntanned face would not be moved for some time to come.

Now was a fine time to cry but I could not. Too overcome by sheer joy, it was time to see my loved ones and thank them for their support. It was time to visit with friends who drove for hours to see us complete this journey. There was just a little time to take in this momentous occasion before we had to move the victory celebration across the road and into the hotel meeting room that Pam had arranged. Did she have any idea what an inspiration and help she was to me? How her trek across America would inspire a journey like ours? I hope so.

She had outdone herself with decorations, an agenda that included time for us to speak, special presentations, food and beverages. The hotel would not allow other celebratory beverages, such as champagne. Pam had collected sand from the Mojave in a glass vial for each of us as well as some other little things to help remind us of our journey. It was a very special time where the team presented Hope For The Warriors a check for $15,000, which was the money that we had raised up to that point. The goal was $30,000 but we were hopeful more contributions would come in upon completion. And they did. We posed for photos, showed our tan lines, and Keith surprised the team with beautiful glass trophies for each of us with our names, the Ride Across USA logo and "3,000 miles" inscribed on them.

After about an hour or so, it was time to get out of our smelly kits and take in our accomplishments individually.

Our spouses were with us and it was time to let the enormity
of what we had done begin to sink in. As we gathered our
bikes and walked them to our own rooms, a feeling of slight
sadness came over me. The team wanted to have "one last
supper" together later that afternoon, so we set a time and
place, overlooking the ocean for the occasion.

Facebook blew up with photos, congratulations, and
messages. Texts poured in too. One that meant so much was
from my son, who simply wrote: "Well done Mom. I'm proud
of you!" My daughter, who is much more expressive, called to
offer congratulations; I could feel the excitement and pride in
her voice. Robin Kelleher from Hope for the Warriors even
texted to thank us.

As I soaked in the tub of my hotel room later, I felt
complete peace and satisfaction that we had completed a life-
changing *and* life-giving event. Was it challenging? It was the
hardest thing I had ever done. Was it frustrating? Yes, a bit
more than I had hoped but not as intense as some rides I have
heard of. Was it easy? In certain portions, particularly with a
nice tailwind. Would I do it again? That remains to be seen.

Week Five Totals
718 miles
23,722' climbing
41H 9M saddle time
Net elevation gain: 0' from ocean to ocean
17.5 mph avg.

Overall Totals
3,058 miles
108,408' climbing
178H 53M saddle time
17.1 mph avg.

14

Moments of Doubt

"Never, never, never give up." (Winston Churchill)

In the chapter "The Countdown Begins" I wrote about a difficult day in April of 2014 when my mind was filled with doubts during a local training ride. While that very low day occurred before the Ride ever commenced, it did not repeat itself as I anticipated it would during our journey. Yes, there were days of frustration and days when I was down on myself (or someone else) but not one moment of any day during our journey did I question what I was doing and why. That DD (Doubt Day) back in April reinforced in me that no matter what I was feeling it was just that -- a feeling. And it reminded me that feelings change. There seems to be two ways to change feelings: (1) with changing circumstances, (2) by reshaping an attitude. Sometimes we can change our immediate surroundings and remove ourselves from the source of our present emotions. Because it is not always possible to control our circumstances, the best solution then is to change our attitude.

I had planned on having a team meeting at the beach house in Malibu to give a pep talk about the prospect of having to declare a Doubt Day for ourselves from time to time. But once we got there and settled in, I didn't feel the need to bring up the subject. As it turned out, it would not be

needed after all because the team didn't have a single DD.
There were moments of doubt that crept in to pay an
unwelcome visit to at least some of our group but I can only
recall two moments when I even heard a teammate in despair.
Just as I never considered giving up, I do not believe that it
crossed the minds of any other team members either. Now was
there a time when I wanted to send someone home? Oh
yes. But not once did I hear murmurings of any of the other
six riders, or our driver, say they wanted to quit. Were there
circumstances we faced that made us think we wanted to quit?
Why certainly. But my belief is that it was a fleeting feeling
and not genuine. How do I know that? Because every single
one of our riders completed the journey -- all 3,058 miles of it.

So as not to paint an unrealistic picture of utopia for
the team, I do need to include a few examples of how hard this
endeavor was at times. As a team, we had several hard days
and a few really hard days. Those were the days that took us to
Tuba City, Arizona; Del Norte, Colorado; La Junta, Colorado;
and Columbus, Georgia. As I reflect on what happened to
make them so difficult, I realized that two of them were
related to the physical challenges of the ride. The other two
were based on team dynamics.

The physical included last-minute route changes to
get us off of very busy highways, but each added some more
climbing and mileage. That didn't bode very well with our
weary bodies, but I took the hit for both of those decisions.
Having heard from local cyclists that the routes we were going
to use were not safe, I went back to the original routes that I
plotted out a year prior to our departure. One of those routes
was Monument, Colorado to La Junta, Colorado. It added
about twenty miles through desolate, windy, desert-like
eastern Colorado, where riding was just plain miserable. While
much safer than riding on Interstate 25 with cars whizzing by
at more than 70 mph, it was not at all a fun day of riding. Most
of us made the best of it but one person rode off the front by

himself for a good couple of hours; perhaps he was dealing with his own frustrations or possibly even moments of doubt. I never did ask.

Another time, I reverted back to an initial route near the end of our trip. We were going through eastern Alabama over to my old stomping grounds in Columbus, Georgia. The original route called for 110 miles and about 5,000 feet of climbing. As Ed was reviewing the routes months before the ride, he had moved the route from MapMyRide to RideWithGPS and it apparently changed the route to take us the most direct way, but on a very dangerous trucking highway. Why did I go back to the original route? Because it was unsafe to ride on a two lane highway with twists, turns and a lot of hills and no shoulder. It was heavily used for logging trucks and eighteen wheelers; it was outright treacherous. Local cyclists and motorists had warned me not to take it. Local drivers knowledgeable about it, including my parents, said they were not comfortable even taking a car on it. In Ed's defense, was unaware of this when he made the changes.

So I advised the team the night before that we should take another route, emailing them the link after getting in late from fireworks. I stayed up a good while, looking over the two routes when the others were in bed. I could tell the next morning that the decision did not go over very well but I felt greatly responsible for our safety, and felt very strongly about staying off US Highway 431. The best thing to do would have been to discuss it over breakfast, but we were going to get on the road at the crack of dawn. I decided to call the shot and deal with any fallout. Sometimes, though, what seems best turns out to cause more harm than good. However, I wish I had called a meeting to get input from the others. Several pairs of eyes looking over a map is always good.

The original route took us on back roads and through the Cheaha State Park and *around* Cheaha Mountain. Joel

Denny, from the Capt. Kyle Comfort Foundation, offered to
escort us to Highway 49 and I said, "Sure. Thank you." I
knew we had to get to Highway 49 but did not realize that
there were two ways to get there: (1) over the eastern edge of
Cheaha Mountain on Skyway Mountain Highway, (2) on
Highway 3 -- the road less traveled and flatter. When Joel told
me, "There's quite a bit of climbing." I retorted with, "That's
OK -- we climbed the Rockies." I did not take his warning all
that seriously; perhaps I should have. He had to have known
that Highway 3 was a bad road or surely he would have taken
us over it instead.

Riding towards Cheaha Mountain. (Photo by Clay Smith)

I'm pretty sure that if the team could have kicked me
off they would have that day. I could see it in their eyes and
feel it in the air. How I wish that they would have seen the
alternative -- US Highway 431 -- and they might have thanked
me. Trusting in your leader is required for something like this;
I just wasn't so confident in their trust. And I didn't feel very
leader-like as the day wore on and one thing after another
seemed to get worse. What happens when the leader is wrong?
It is always difficult to admit making mistakes. I second-

guessed it numerous times that day but chose to press on since we were committed and we had split up by noon.

The route leaving Oxford was a pretty country road and it began winding up and up around Mile Ten or so. Joel stayed right in front of us and slowly led the way. It didn't take long for Scott to tell me, "My Garmin says we are off course." I replied that "Joel knows where to go; he lives out here." Before too long we are really climbing and the group was split up. Now please understand that I am a little "off" to some people. Because I love climbing and the challenge of getting up mountains, I can be a bit insensitive to others who do not share the same enthusiasm. We knew that we would have several thousand feet of climbing to do, but the gradients that faced us this day were a surprise to everyone. It didn't take long for me to realize that this particular section of the day's route was going to take its toll on us. I tried to keep a positive attitude but in the back of my mind I wondered what the team may be plotting to do to me in my sleep.

After a good hour or so of steep climbs and thrilling descents I cheerily announced to all those around to "think of this as a character-building ride!" Hmmm ... that didn't go over so well. This was not a good time to be Perky Polly and the timing was poor on my part. They failed to see the humor in my words. My intention was really to try and lighten the mood a bit. Sometimes I am not such a good judge of when to close my mouth. More encouraging words would have fared better than a flippant comment.

My sister had joined us for two days and her fresh legs could climb better than all of us on that unseasonably cool Alabama morning. However, she had a minor hand injury that made it uncomfortable to hold the handlebars. In one way or another, we were all uncomfortable, whether physically or mentally. So she was in good company.

Two hours into this ride we found ourselves on Alabama Highway 49 on the way to Lineville, Alabama, where the road surface was chip seal. Yuck. In case you are unfamiliar with it, it is like riding on the top of Rice Krispy Treats that turned to concrete. The smoothest portion of the road was a six-inch-wide margin on either side of the yellow line, so we rode it as long as traffic was absent. Scott, Leigh and I found ourselves together and we were a good group. Three others were ahead and two were behind. Our escort did his job to get us this far and we did not see him again for another hour or so. On Highway 49 I cracked a joke that the road could not get any worse and that soon the roughness would be behind us. Boy was I wrong. Hadn't I learned that this was not a good day for jokes?

The team regrouped at a barbecue restaurant. We met up with my Dad and brother-in-law and then said goodbye to our guides Joel and Nancy. It was a nice lunch break and we were all a bit tired from the terrain and bad road surface. Not long after rolling out of Lineville, construction signs appeared. The road surface suddenly changed from decent to almost unbearable. The asphalt had been scraped up and replaced by billions of large dimples. Indeed the road could get worse, and had. About six miles of bumpy, torn up, rough road accompanied us and I again uttered something along the lines of: "It really cannot get worse than this." I wanted to believe this and it was no joke.

A short turn off that road took us to a shady, scenic lane that happened to be pocked with water-filled potholes. Scott reported that his Garmin had us on course so we zigged and zagged on other old, beaten up country roads that were supposedly going to get us back to a main road, which maybe, just maybe, would be smooth.

Nope. Not a chance. The road all but disintegrated after one right turn and the surface was almost as bad as Route 66 in the middle of the baking Mojave Desert. It was so bad, in fact, that my sister chose to get in the SAG and wait until conditions improved. Her hand was throbbing. Scott and I

continued on the Road from Hades as his Garmin promised
that in three more miserable miles we would be introduced to
a little highway. Thankfully, that proved to be accurate and we
stopped to meet up with the SAG on a normal road. We
ingested a little nutrition (that is what I called my Snickers bar
and Dr. Pepper treat). We also visited with a few locals before
resuming our ride. It was so great to have those horrific roads
behind us. Surely we would find smooth roads ahead as we
returned to civilization. Unfortunately this is where Leigh and
I got separated because of miscommunication among the
group as to which road to take to Columbus. Clay insisted on
Highway 431 and Scott's Garmin dictated a different route.
Leigh was with Ed and Marion and I knew she would be fine
as long as those three stuck together. Hopefully we would
meet up soon.

Sometimes ignorance is bliss. We rode on .... and
on..... and on for what seemed like endless miles to nowhere.
Our total miles for the day were expected to be about 120.
Add in the elevation and it was going to be a torturous day.
There was no other way around it; this part of Alabama had
lots of hills. After crossing Interstate 85 and nearing Opelika,
Alabama, I knew that we were not too far from my hometown
of Columbus, which was our destination for the night. Clay
called to inform us that Ruth notified him that "Road 26 was
dirt." Road 26? That had to be incorrect as all road numbers
around these parts were triple digits. Another twenty minutes
of riding took us to the middle of nowhere and we found
ourselves on County Road 326. You can figure out what
happened from here.

Another half mile up the road, it did indeed change to
a dirt road. As our day was going, you know it couldn't just be
a dirt road. It was a sandy dirt road full of rocks, sticks and
even hills. At one point the sand was so deep and loose that
Scott dismounted and walked his bike for a few yards. I
decided to turn it into a challenge and dared myself to not

unclip or fall over. It was not easy and I felt my back wheel
slide out from under me more than a couple of times. Two
miles of this was just about too much after the long day we
had. By now it was after noon. Five plus hours of riding had
gotten us within thirty miles of the end of the day's route. The
challenge was difficult but I didn't allow myself to think of
giving up. There was no doubt that we were going to be done
with these dastardly roads -- just not soon enough.

After many more hills and miles, the team had
reunited at the hotel in time for dinner. Our exhausted bodies
and tired minds had enough; the day was very long, pretty hot
and finally done. One Garmin showed we had climbed almost
8,000 feet and ridden 121 miles. Thanks to a donation from
First Baptist Church of Columbus, we had a very nice hotel
for the night and some good grub awaiting us close by. Our
team was weary, but no one complained. We simply picked yet
another Mexican restaurant for dinner and made our way over.
Our crowd swelled to fifteen people with my family, Steve
Barto and Catherine Bradshaw, from Fort Benning, who had
arranged for us to ride with some wounded warriors the next
morning. One would never have known that our team had
faced such a rough day; moods were light and there was no
shortage of laughter as stories were shared. Any frustration
from the hard day did not show up at the dinner table.

Just as my original DD caught me off guard before
the ride ever began, the couple of doubtful times that followed
caught me by surprise because the doubts that came into play
had nothing to do with physically being able to complete the
ride. They had everything to do with doubts in other areas: my
leadership, my choices, my reactions at times and my ability
to respond to other team members' expectations. The doubts
never once made me want to quit the ride -- only to improve as
a leader and as a human being. In hindsight I should have
called these "MOD" for "moments of doubt" rather than a
whole day of doubt. Thankfully, they never lasted more than a

few hours and never ruined an entire day.

We all have doubts about jobs, parenting, marriage, and long-ago choices. Those thoughts can blindside us. Should we despise them? Should we deny them? While self-preservation screams out to us to abandon what is uncomfortable, we become stronger by standing firm and growing from these situations. Sometimes what may feel like a shroud of doubt can become just a few moments of hesitation that make us stop and consider what is happening. It is important to identify the feeling as well as what is truth in the situation. Truth triumphs feelings when we remove the emotion from a given situation. While not easy to do, it is a practice we can incorporate to deal with self-doubt. As long as we allow the doubt to consume us, we will live accordingly and be defeated. Who wants to live in that state? Not me.

A valuable lesson: Turn the doubts and fears into an impetus for change by recounting the truth and moving on from there. With so many miles to ride that day, I had plenty of time to reflect on what had occurred and what was still transpiring along the way. There were moments when I stuffed emotion into my back pocket and others when it faced me square on. What would I do differently next time? Not carry the full burden of feeling responsible for the whole team. Call a meeting and ask for their input. I would let go of the fear of wondering what everyone else was thinking and open the lines of communication sooner. It was clear that the day by day toll of riding so much and so hard was beginning to add up. This was new territory and we all needed to give each other a bit of a break.

There were just three more days of riding, and the belief that we would succeed was becoming more apparent.

15

Team Members' Reflections

*"Teamwork is the ability to work together toward a
common vision. The ability to direct individual
accomplishments toward organizational objectives. It is
the fuel that allows common people to attain uncommon
results."* (Andrew Carnegie)

While this work is my perspective of our journey and written through my heart and eyes, it is important to remember that this is simply my story. There were six other riders and three SAG assistants, each of whom has his or her own perspective. I invited all to share their thoughts in this closing chapter and several responded. Several others wholeheartedly agreed with Scott's synopsis and said they had nothing else to add. I trust you will enjoy reading about the ride from a few other points of view and in their own words.

Scott Manning

The journey was so wonderful from so many prospectives.

The first prospective was seeing the USA. I tell people if they really want to see America, the best way is at twenty miles per hour. Each day we had a chance to view the subtle changes in the landscape, people, food, local animals as the group rode east. Each day, there was always small changes and it was really a lot of fun watching for them and discovering them. I had a perception that the Midwest would be boring to ride through, but I was wrong in this perception. I really enjoyed the Midwest, especially Kansas. If I was going to list my favorite states, they would be California, Arizona, Colorado, and Kansas. I think the day of rain and the Ozark Hills in Missouri might have damped my love for Missouri. I still believe the term "Ozark" is Indian for "Death by a thousand hills" and I still recall that ride and thinking a good bulldozer could have flatten those hills out. I found the "Zippy" engine did not work as well on small hills as it did on the larger and longer hills. When we got into the southern states, this was cool, but I had ridden in many of these states before so there was less amazement and sense of discovery.

On a physical level, I was nervous about physically doing a century ride every day. I knew that I could ride a few back-to-back centuries. But doing thirty one of them almost back to back is a different story. Doing the ride has instilled a new sense of confidence in my riding. I am more able to taking on major challenges with more confidence and I know how to plan for long rides and ensure their success. When I did the 1000 km ride a few weeks ago, that was a challenge to do in three days, but how could a person who rode across the US fail to finish only a 1000 km ride? I am looking forward to the 1200 km in 2015 and doing that in four days. After the 1000-km ride, I was back on the bike two days later riding some recovery-paced rides.

From a group perspective, I know we had some challenging moments, but we worked through them and made sure we all succeeded. I tell everyone that every cyclist rode 100 percent of every mile, from shore to shore. There was never one idea of hopping in the car and riding to the next town. We all wanted the achievement of saying "we cycled

100 percent of the US" and we did it as a team. I know each
cyclist had a different set of challenging days during the
ride. For me, it was the Ozarks. Marion mentioned the hills on
the way to Williams Arizona was her challenging day. I think
the 150-mile ride across the eastern Colorado was a challenge
for the entire team. But the cool part was that we worked
together and finish each day's ride out successfully and
without injuries. To me, success meant "coming into that day's
finish without injury or broken bike and still able to ride the
next day."

From the food prospective, I loved eating at all of the
local places and tasting the local foods. Having ice cream so
often was a real treat and I need to thank Keith for enforcing
the "must have ice cream daily" rule. I have never eaten so
much in my life and still come back 5 pounds lighter. I know
Marion's gluten issue was a major benefit for me (Thank you
Marion!). The "Zippy" engine needed a lot of carbs to keep it
running smoothly. I still benefit from her gluten issue in the
1000 km ride where she could not eat the flour wrap at
McDonalds. I could not see that going to waste. I will always
sit next to Marion at restaurants

My final perspective was how generous people were
to us and the H4W charity. It was really amazing to see people
open up their homes, churches, communities centers for the
team and to help this charity. The people who donated along
the trip were really amazing. We only had to tell them why we
were riding and people opened their wallets up. The
motorcycle, police and fire truck escorts were really awesome.
It was really a lot of fun being escorted into a town by some
emergency vehicle. It almost seemed like we were riding in a
parade at 20 mph and I have never ridden in a parade before. I
also found that I loved chasing and trying to catch the vehicle
that was escorting the team in. This sense of "chase" is strong
in me and I thought of the greyhound at a dog track trying to
run the rabbit. I know the greyhound will never catch that

rabbit and Keith pointed out to me that I will never catch the vehicle in front of me. They will just speed up. I coined the term "greyhound effect" to describe this chase desire and the inability to catch the target.

It was a great pleasure to ride and spend time with everyone. I really had a good time with everyone and there were some truly funny moments along the trip. Spending time at breakfast, lunch, dinner, riding, midday ice cream snack and even sleeping together was fun. Overall it was a journey of a lifetime and I hope to do more of these trips, but I know the next adventures will never be as special as this trip was.

Ruth D'Aiuto

I knew before leaving that I could do this. I did not care how hard it would be. I just didn't think about that or pain. For me, physical pain is easier to bear than emotional pain. Having been diagnosed and treated for breast cancer and going through a difficult divorce was much harder than this would be. I've done more than 760 miles and over 35,000 feet of climbing in a few days and knew 100 miles a day for 31 would be a dream. One day at a time. One foot over the other.

I had been to all of these states and seen so much of where we had ridden by car or motor home with my kids as they were growing up. I never traveled as a child so when I had mine I wanted to give them the world. And we did. I didn't like flying because I always got air sick. I also felt like I missed out on what was in between here and there. I always chose to drive wherever it was we needed to be. I didn't want to miss anything. No matter the miles, we drove. The opportunity to do it with friends by two wheels was mind boggling.

The chance to see all these places at a relaxed pace was such a blessing. To take pictures and share in once in a lifetime experiences, like Monument Valley, was a blessing.

Words cannot really describe how a heart changes on a trip like this. You learn about yourself and others in a totally different way.

I already knew I was a rider who preferred to ride alone or in silence. I'm not a rider who likes to communicate while moving on a bike. I'm a thinker during this time. Before or after riding I'm social but during the ride I found it hard to talk.

Being together 24/7 brings out the good and the bad in all of us. I'm not sure if it's good or bad that we were all mainly acquaintances before the ride. I think it may have made it easier. If we had known each other on a deeper more vulnerable level, I wonder how it would have changed the dynamics. But when we were done, we went about our lives. Kind of strange that it didn't bond us deeper but it does make us have one thing in common that so few share: an incredible, sometimes indescribable 35 days.

I also wanted to say something about riding with my coach and best friend Keith, and thank the Lord for his grace and protection!

Clay Smith

As I reflect back on the trip today, it seems so long ago. And I have nothing but fond memories. I especially remember picking you all up at LAX and spending three fun days living together in our rented house on the Malibu Beach. It was a great start for this epic journey. It was surreal to me as I used to patrol that area as a Santa Monica Police Officer for twenty five years. Getting to ride with my two boys on the bike path along the Pacific Ocean was a real special treat for me.

I want to thank Tracy for allowing me the opportunity to be part of this team. What these cyclists accomplished was nothing short of miraculous in my mind. Doing a century ride is one thing, but doing it day in and day out without any real drama is something else.

I'll never forget the generosity and support shown by the people we meet along the way. The motorcade coming into Kingman, Kansas. The police escorts. The lady in Pratt, Kansas sitting down at a table where we were having lunch and unceremoniously giving us a check for $1,000, as did one of my high school classmates.

Driving cross country at 20 mph might seem slow to some people, but the time seemed to fly by. I'm ready to do it again. It was a great experience, a great bunch of men and women, and a great cause.

God bless America.

Clay Smith

Pam Hunt

Remember your first bike? Remember how it felt to ride as fast as you could for as far as you could? Remember the giddy exuberance of flying down a hill? The exhilarating sensation of the wind hitting your face? The freedom of knowing that you could go anywhere your legs could take you?

People sit around and dream but don't try to fulfill their potential. I am very proud of Team Ride Across USA for fulfilling a dream and having their legs take them across this great country.

After I finished my bike adventure in 2005, I took a USA road map and traced out my route. I am still amazed that I accomplished this ride but remember the thrills, people, and smells I encountered along the way. People often asked how I was able to do it. I replied that I went for a bike ride every day but slept in a different bed every night.

Congratulations to all of you and may your memories be as happy as mine.

16

Dream It. Live It.

"Success is not final, failure is not fatal: it is the courage to continue that counts." (Winston Churchill)

Thirty six days and thousands of miles after aiming our wheels eastward from the Pacific Ocean, I woke up in the hotel at the beach feeling a little empty, a little lost. There was no team meeting, no route to consider, no story to hear. As an early riser, I left BillyD in bed and went to breakfast alone. A new reality was presenting itself -- life after the Ride Across. What would I do now without the infinite details that kept me awake night after night for the past two-plus years? The business of writing thank you notes and wrapping up financial records that now lie before me are nothing compared with the enormity of pre-ride preparations. The most daring dream of my life was now accomplished. What next? I find myself at an unsettled place and it feels a bit uneasy.

A dream realized is bittersweet. The overwhelming feeling of accomplishment teeters with a daunting emptiness that demands to be filled. Similar to other situations in life, there is a choice to be made: to propel forward despite not knowing what lies ahead or to be idle and wait for what may be coming my way. The answer is easy: Keep pressing forward in faith.

Many times in my life I have been faced with one dream ending and another waiting to be presented. Most of the time the next desire lies unidentified in the shadows until the tapestry of life presents itself ready to receive it. Now it is time to move forward yet again, integrating the highs and lows of this journey into other parts of my life. The chords of broken dreams have been woven together from childhood and are now being reshaped into a life that promises new dreams. You see, disappointments of the past often turn into magnificent works of art in the future, if you look for them.

Negative Events Need Not Define Us for Life

Long ago, my mother had warned me to "never get alone with a boy," and for good reason. At the time I did not comprehend her warning, nor take it very seriously. She knew boys better than I did and I was a pretty naive young teen. Without going into detail, the events of the summer between eighth and ninth grades really did a number on me for many years of my life. What happened was out of the blue and out of my control, and I lived with it secretly until I was twenty eight years old. From age fourteen until around thirty five, this horrible shame that harbored itself in my mind and spirit seemed to rule over me. Self doubt reigned within me, and while I could put on a happy face to cover up most of the pain, the consequences of unhealthy choices made during these years came at a high price.

Many -- dare I say most -- of the doubts that whisper in my ear even today stem from these events. At times scar tissue in my emotional heart shows itself when I allow those doubts to taunt me again. For example, when someone on our Ride questioned my ability as a leader, it pierced me deeply. My confidence waivered as I heard those dark, evil voices again trying to entice me to be afraid. When my body was crying out in pain in Kansas the voices reminded me of many failures.

But then ... just as boldly as those voices spoke, every single time I called on God for help, He reminded me of Truth. And the Truth is that I will not allow past negative circumstances define who I am today. Truth is that I have grown past the terrible things that occurred that summer and beyond. Truth is that I am whole, healthy and have chosen to move on. Truth is that I do not have to believe those voices.

These are the other truths that this Ride carved deeply into the folds of my heart.

Truth: Patriotism is alive and well in the USA

One of the many beautiful aspects of our journey was to see that, from Coast to Coast, people love our great nation. There were flags painted on barns across the Midwest, flying high on cabins in the Rockies, and stuck in front yards of Small Town, USA. At Red, White and Boom in Mount Vernon, Missouri, American flags waved by the thousands all over the county fairgrounds. Dozens of Old Glories lined the streets of Central Alabama as we rolled through on July Fourth. As we exchanged our smelly, dirty kits for our clean, white Ride Across USA T-shirts at dinner time, we always garnered smiles and heard: "Thank you for what you are doing." Despite the political climate of our day, regardless of party or politics that played out in Washington as we rode, the people of the United States of America were supportive and grateful.

I encourage you not to believe those who try and say that patriotism is dead. They have not seen America as I have. Maybe some need to get their heads out of the partisan stew and take a tour of the great country that we call our own. Perhaps Clay stated it best when he said with tear-filled eyes, "My faith in America has been renewed." Amen brother. Small Town America is vibrant, patriotic and still full of those who believe in our nation and her dreams.

Truth: It takes courage to dream

With so many miles to think as we pedaled close to 180 hours, I could not help but think of those we were riding for. How have their lives changed post-war? What dreams do they have? Did their injuries kill the dream or simply put it on hold? Pictures flashed in my mind of military veterans that were racing as hand cyclists zooming their way through the streets of Tampa last spring at a Criterium race I went to watch. I was in awe of their tenacity, attacking the corners like nobody's business, racing all-out on these ground-level machines with no holds barred. Teeth gritting, sweat dripping and knuckles gripping the cranks as if their very lives depended on crossing that finish line. Those are the ones who chose to continue dreaming.

But many do not. Many left their dreams on the battlefield or buried them with their buddy who lost his life in the Middle East. Many do not believe in dreams. Some may fear them. But all should be given the opportunity to dare to dream.

One impressive soldier told me a bit of his story as we rode away from the Infantry Museum at Fort Benning, Georgia. He had been overseas and in battle. He saw some horrors of war and is now in the War Transition Unit at Benning, getting his life back in order. As we pedaled side by side he told me with a very serious tone in his voice and emotion on his face, "Cycling has saved my life." It has given him confidence, purpose, pleasure and freedom from dark thoughts that were trying to occupy his mind. He told me: "When I get on my bike it is like my problems roll away." The smile he flashed as he said that was evidence that hope remains. A life restored ... amazing.

Maybe you cannot relate to life-changing obstacles.

Maybe you have a different kind of emotional injury: abuse or victimization, divorce, death of a loved one. Perhaps your injury came from someone who didn't believe in you and beat you down so that you have lost faith in yourself.

Truth: My dream became reality

"Dreams are illustrations from the book your soul is writing about you." (Marsha Norman)

This is still sinking in. It hits me at different times but often as a tidal wave of emotion. As I flew out to Colorado for Parent's Weekend at the Academy last August I was hit with such a swell as I looked out the window at an elevation of 35,000 feet and said quietly to myself, "That's a lot of land down there, and my legs propelled me all the way across it." No doubt the man next to me wondered why I had to wipe away a tear or two while I stared out the window at Kansas below. He didn't bother to ask but he knew something was moving me. I was in no mood to answer because I most likely would have burst into tears.

Moments like that come and go more frequently now than when we first returned. Upon returning to our little hometown, life as usual resumed. Being busy with work, family, writing, organizing the Mount Dora Bicycle Festival for October kept the days full. I kept telling myself that the realization would sink in, if only I would slow down. That must be why it hits in spurts. With both successful events behind me now, I can relax, watch videos of our ride, close my eyes and reminisce. We had some wonderful and remarkable times that I don't want to slip away.

My dream became reality. As I listen to others, converse with them and take mental notes from overheard conversations in daily life, I wonder how many people can honestly make that statement their own? How many people do you know who have had a dream, set out to accomplish it and actually done so? Perhaps the most poignant part of this dream began with thought: Dare to dream. I believe that is what stops most people ... not being willing to take a dare, for whatever reason.

Truth: Everyone can dream
"You have to dream before your dreams can come true."
(A. P. J. Abdul Kalam)

Maybe that is where it will begin for you -- with a dare. OK. I dare you. Turn off the devices, get away from the television, put down this book and close your eyes. Allow your mind to take you where you think you cannot go. Why not? Perhaps you are in the way of your own dream. No excuses. Just dream. Allow yourself to do something in your mind that you are not sure your body can handle. And if I may implore you even more -- add others to your dream. Share it with someone or help out a cause. Why not? Something my Dad often repeated: We all have enough time and money to do what we really want to do.

Not too long ago I was talking with my hairdresser

about the Ride. She said to me in all seriousness, "I could never do anything like that, Tracy." What flashed in my mind and out of my mouth was this, "You know Jackie, the difference in our dreams is that I totally believed I could. And you can too, if you believe it."

"The future belongs to those who believe in the beauty of their dreams." (Eleanor Roosevelt)

First of all one must dream. Secondly, one must believe that it actually will come true. A favorite verse from the New Testament is this:

"Faith is being sure of what we hope for and certain of what we do not see." (Hebrews 11:1)

I believed that I would complete the cross country journey. I was sure that we would impact the lives of others. I knew my dream would come to fruition. How did I know? By faith: The uncomplicated belief in my God's leadership, provision and protection. Faith is what will get you through when self-doubt comes rushing in.

Truth: We all have a sphere of influence in our lives

Unbeknownst to me as I was planning the Ride, this dream was going to make an impact on the lives of many. This was a truly humbling lesson framing everything touching our mission. While I had hoped to make a difference for some people, I was unprepared for what else came.

Friends, acquaintances, strangers, clients, family members, friends of my children, and my social media friends began telling me how inspiring it was to read about the mission. We met people in every state who talked with us at rest stops, in restaurants and even at restroom-break stops. They were astounded that we were pulling off such a feat. Many more were touched by the fact that we were riding to raise awareness for Hope for the Warriors. They pulled out their billfolds to donate. Quite a few wanted photos with us and pledged to donate online.

We heard stories of injured family members who had lost their own battle with PTS (post-traumatic stress) or lost their lives in combat. Our sphere of influence was growing and, rather than feeling afraid of it, I decided to embrace it and make the most of it. Every time we had an opportunity to talk with the press I did, no matter how weary the mind or body was. We were a voice to be heard and were all so humbled that others wanted to hear about our mission. To be able to inspire others is a wondrous gift and responsibility. Clay, Scott and Bill were each interviewed several times (the others may have been a bit camera shy). And each had their own perspective of our mission. It was fantastic to see them embrace the multiple opportunities to share our cause.

"All men dream, but not equally. Those who dream by night in the dusty recesses of their minds, wake in the day to find that it was vanity: but the dreamers of the day are dangerous men, for they may act on their dreams with open eyes, to make them possible." (T. E. Lawrence)

Truth: Live It for Others

It has taken almost three years to check off some significant items on my Live It list: Racing for Ricky, Ride Across USA and now, writing a book. It is time to add some new goals to the list, and I have been giving it a good bit of thought. Both physical and intellectual challenges are luring me this time. Some of these dreams are more fun than others, but all share a key element -- the mindset of inviting others to join in. Yes, I have some more items for the Live It list, and I hope to continually add to it as I am able to check off feats that I have accomplished. For example, I want to ride a century ride of 100 miles in all fifty states. So far I have done nine, thanks to our Ride. And last November, I added South Carolina. Forty more to go. Perhaps I can gather some friends to join me as we knock off one state at a time. Who knows what the future holds, but I have an idea that others will like this next Live It list concept.

Do you have a Bucket List? What if you kicked it to the curb and start your Live It list? Dream, plan, and honor someone else along the way. Ride your bike. Walk a 5K event. Climb a mountain. Do something that is challenging. The ideas of things you can do to impact in this world are endless. Start with a dream that has significant goals and challenges. Plan for obstacles to appear, then plan on overcoming them. You will find that, by the end, you have not only made a difference in someone else's life, but you have become a better person in the process. You just may be surprised how your dreams can -- and will-- affect change in others' lives.

Revisiting the television reporter's question from Day Thirty Three: *How has this ride changed me*? It has given me courage to continue dreaming. I desire to cultivate an attitude of overlooking my own shortcomings and those of others around me. I would like to be a bit more gracious when troubles arise and learn the full story, rather than making a judgement. My hope is to continue to release insecurities that I used to let get the best of me. I have had to practice the discipline of making decisions and standing by them -- even if it means having to eat a little crow for it. That counts for some kind of growth. By spending hours a day in thought is a sure way to get to know yourself better. There were some things that I found that I did not like, and I resolved to grow from them. Maybe during the next dream fulfillment, I will be able to say that I have indeed risen above those things. In reality, I'm just likely to find more new things to work on. That is okay by me, for should the time come when I think I have arrived, I am in trouble.

With this ambitious feat behind me, it is incredibly exciting to wonder what lies ahead on the horizon. There are some new things that I have put on an updated Live It list. Some things I want to do are: Reach the summit of Pikes Peak by bike; Climb Alpe d'Huez in France; Seek other challenges and ask: "Why not?" In keeping with the Live It theme, each of these rides will be done in honor or memory of another.

Most of all, I hope to inspire others to Live It and to help others achieve their dreams. Just recently, someone I met at a cycling event in South Carolina last November invited me to join his crew team for his solo Race Across America (RAAM). What a wonderful opportunity to help this man fulfill his dream. After some thought and discussion with my husband, I agreed and will now spend two weeks this summer going cross country – over some of the same roads that we traversed in our Ride. Wolf Creek Pass lies in wait for us yet again; how exciting to be able to support someone else over it this time.

Even without a diagnosis of some sort, our time on Earth is really pretty short. My ultimate goal in life is to make a difference in this world. To know that I can contribute to society as I set out personal goals is an epiphany for me. I am really nothing special or out of the ordinary. There is nothing that I have done that others cannot and have not done. The difference is this: Some believe. We are no better than others; we simply believe. Sometimes we have no defined reason to believe, no evidence to substantiate our thought process, yet faith is there.

When Pam Hunt shared her story with me about her cross-country ride, why on earth would I ever adhere to the bizarre notion that I could do it too? Because she ended her story as I will mine: "If I can do it, anybody can!"

Facts and Figures

- As much as 93,000 calories per person, which is the equivalent of 26.5 pounds. It's also 212 Dairy Queen hot fudge sundaes per team member.
- 108,980' climbed = scaling Mount Everest 3.7 times
- The team went through 30+ tubes and 3 tires between us all
- Pedal strokes: approximately 1,700,000 times our knees flexed and pushed down on the pedals
- Raised $22,000+ for Hope For The Warriors
- We dined at Mexican restaurants so many times that a few team members have vowed "never again!"
- As a team we lost about 60 pounds during our 5 weeks of riding
- We went through 10 states: California, Arizona, Colorado, Kansas, Missouri, Arkansas, Tennessee, Alabama, Georgia, Florida
- Longest day in the saddle: Monument, Colorado to La Junta, Colorado- 155 miles
- Shortest day: Woodland Park, Colorado to Monument, Colorado - 55 miles, 4,000+ feet of climbing
- Hottest day: Needles, California –122 degrees
- Coldest day: Bayfield, Colorado 38 degrees at the start
- Average time in the saddle every day -- about six and one half hours

- Number of days over 100 miles --17 (over half of our riding days)
- Number of rain days -- 1
- Number of riders who said they wanted to quit -- 0
- Biggest wind: going into Kansas. Weather.com reported 36 mph that day.

Team member Bill came up with some of his own statistics (printed with permission)
- Our climbing is about equal to climbing 8,600 flights of stairs or 85 times up (and DOWN) the Empire State Building
- Riding for 177.23 hours. My average heart rate was 107 bpm that is 1,137,817 heartbeats
- At 17.4 average mph it would take 60 days to circumnavigate the Earth at the equator. We went 1/8th of the way.
- Burning 64,000 calories in 177.223 hours is 362 calories/hour
- Pasta -- about 90 pounds of spaghetti
- Cliff Bars -- about 280 bars

Glossary

AquaBike -- An endurance event where participants swim for a specified distance then bike afterward. Distances vary as with triathlon events. In AquaBike there is no run portion.

Bibs -- Cycling shorts with mesh straps that go over the shoulders to help keep the shorts in place.

Buzzed --When a car comes too close to cyclists on the road. Some states have a three-foot law to protect cyclists from motorists passing too closely.

Carbon fork --The part of the frame that holds the front wheel and that is turned to steer; made of carbon fiber in newer road bikes.

Century --A ride that is 100 miles long.

Chamois -- A lubricating substance that cyclists put in their cycling shorts to help reduce chafing

Criterium -- A bike race held on a short course (usually less than 1 mile), often run on closed-off city center streets. Also called a "crit."

Draft -- The airstream created by a cyclist directly in front of you.

Echelon -- A line of riders seeking maximum drafting in a crosswind, resulting in a diagonal line across the road.

Grades -- The pitch or slope of a hill or mountain.

Kit -- An outfit consisting of a jersey and matching shorts or bibs; uniform

Metric century --A 62.5-mile ride. Metric centuries are often offered along with the standard 100-mile century on organized group rides.

Olympic Distance -- An endurance event (triathlon or aquabike) with distances of 1500 meters for the swim, 40 kilometer bike and 10 kilometer run segments

Paceline -- Group of riders riding at high speed by drafting one another. Riders will take turns at the front to break the wind, then rotate to the back of the line to rest in the draft. Larger group rides will often form double pacelines with two columns of riders.

Road race -- Cycling racing event that ranges from several kilometers to up to 200 kilometers.

SAG -- Support And Gear; a vehicle that transports tools,

parts, nutrition, hydration and support for a group of riders.
Sprint triathlon -- An endurance event consisting of three segments. Swim portion about 400 meters, bike 20 kilometers and run is normally 5 kilometers.
Credit: Wikipedia